Black Voices
from Reconstruction

BLACK VOICES
from
RECONSTRUCTION

1865–1877

J O H N   D A V I D   S M I T H

The Millbrook Press
Brookfield, Connecticut

Photographs courtesy of The T.W. Wood Art Gallery, Montpelier, Vt.:
p. 13; Library of Congress: pp. 32–33, 104; Bettmann: p. 46; The
Schomburg Center, New York Public Library: pp. 53, 112, 115, 120, 124,
136; Special Collections, The University of Texas at El Paso Library: p.
58; National Museum of American Art, Smithsonian Institution/Art
Resource, NY: p. 67; The Metropolitan Museum of Art, Gift of Erving
and Joyce Wolf, 1982: p. 86; North Wind Picture Archives: pp. 95, 149.

Library of Congress Cataloging-in-Publication Data
Smith, John David, 1949–
Black voices from Reconstruction, 1865–1877 / John David Smith.
p.   cm.
Includes bibliographical references and index.
Summary: Original source documents are woven into a narrative
providing the experiences and points of view of former slaves during
the long process of Reconstruction following the Civil War.
ISBN 1-56294-583-1 (lib. bdg.)
1. Afro-Americans—History—1863–1877—Sources—Juvenile
literature.   2. Afro-Americans—Southern States—History—Sources
—Juvenile literature.   3. Reconstruction—Sources—Juvenile
literature.   [1. Afro-Americans—History—1863–1877.
2. Reconstruction—Sources.]   I. Title.
E185.2.S66   1996
973′.0496073—dc20   95-47465   CIP   AC

for Rodney E. Sheratsky—
teacher, friend, exemplar

Contents

Acknowledgments

Many years ago I had a marvelous high school teacher who inspired me to become a professor and author. He radiated enthusiasm for teaching, demanded the highest quality of scholarship, and maintained a delightful sense of humor. Dr. Rodney E. Sheratsky has influenced my professional life profoundly, and I dedicate *Black Voices from Reconstruction* to him.

I met Dr. Jennifer Fleischner when I lectured at the Du Bois Institute at Harvard University in 1993. She suggested that I write a book for young adult readers and put me in contact with The Millbrook Press. I am grateful for her encouragement and for her interest in my work. My editors at The Millbrook Press, Kate Nunn and Deborah Cannarella, have been most helpful in getting this book published.

Three of my graduate students at North Carolina State University—Beth L. Calamia, Daniel J. Salemson, and Yvette M. Stillwell—provided valuable research assistance in the preparation of this book. The Reference and Interlibrary Loan departments at D. H. Hill Library cheerfully and efficiently enabled me to locate texts. Drs. Suzanne Chester, Jeffrey J. Crow, William C. Harris, and Antony H. Harrison helped me find materials, answered questions, and read drafts of the manuscript.

Closer to home Alex, Lisa, and Lorenz seemed pleased that I finally would write a book that a teenager might want to read. Sylvia listened patiently and lovingly cheered the project on in every way.

Introduction

In 1861 the southern states contained four million black slaves—men, women, and children. The ancestors of these blacks came to North America by way of the Caribbean. Over two centuries the Africans became African Americans and by the eve of the Civil War composed almost one third of the South's population.

The black slaves were property. They belonged legally to their white masters. The slaves not only were owned but also were worked, hired, sold, traded, even insured. They were not allowed to move freely without a written pass provided by their masters. Slaves could not marry legally, carry weapons, learn to read or write, or conduct business. When they ran away with hopes of reaching the North—and freedom—they commonly were hunted down by slave catchers who were armed with guns and bloodhounds.

Following Abraham Lincoln's election in 1860, white southerners feared that Lincoln and the Republicans would destroy slavery and their "southern way of life." In response, in February 1861, white southerners established a new government, the Confederate States of America. Determined to maintain a slaveholding republic and to leave the Union, the Confederates declared their independence. Lincoln refused to recognize the right of secession, and in April 1861, the Confederates attacked Fort Sumter, a U.S. military installation at Charleston, South Carolina. A state of insurrection, or rebellion, existed, Lincoln said, on the part of the disloyal southern states, and the President began to suppress the uprising.

Four years later, after more than 620,000 men (360,000 northerners and as many as 260,000 southerners) had died in the bloody Civil War, the Confederacy lay in ruins and the slaves stood free. Ironically, the war that had begun to protect the right of white southerners to own slaves ended with slavery's destruction. During the conflict, southern slaves worked for their masters but remained hopeful that the war would result in their liberation. In fact, some slaves aided the Yankees by serving as scouts, by destroying their masters' crops, and by performing their agricultural labor slowly and inefficiently.

Almost 180,000 free blacks fought valiantly in the U.S. Colored Troops to free their black brothers and sisters. The use of black troops was a dramatic change in policy by the Lincoln administration. Though many whites doubted that blacks would be able soldiers, black troops proved themselves worthy of the challenge. They distinguished themselves in battles at Port Hudson, Milliken's Bend, Fort Wagner, and numerous others. As Union troops penetrated the Confederacy, slaves flocked to their camps to be free. Many joined the northern troops. Historians refer to this process as wartime emancipation. By the end of the war more than 2,700 black soldiers were killed in action and 17 received the Medal of Honor for gallantry in combat. According to historian Dudley Taylor Cornish, "As a soldier in the Union Army, the American Negro proved his manhood and established a strong claim to equality of treatment and opportunity."[1]

The slaves received their freedom several ways. Confederate slaves were freed during the war by Lincoln's Emancipation Proclamation in January 1863. Many others were liberated by the Union troops as they conquered the South. Those in Delaware

A Southern Cornfield *by Thomas Waterman Wood, 1861.*

and Maryland were freed by specific laws called manumission statutes. Slaves held by Unionists within the Confederacy and in the loyal border states (Missouri and Kentucky) were set free by the Thirteenth Amendment in December 1865. Finally, after more than two centuries as slaves, blacks finally were free. Their long-awaited day of "jubilo," the term that slaves used for "jubilee," had arrived.

Union victory in the war settled two things: Never again would states try to leave the union and never again would people be enslaved in the United States. But despite their emancipation, the future of the South's freed men and women remained unsettled. Their political, social, and economic status remained hazy. Though legally "free," they faced an uncertain future. Many encountered harsh treatment by their liberators, the Union troops, and by their former masters. Some considered the immediate fruits of freedom to be bitter indeed. As Reconstruction unfolded, blacks had many questions. How would the two races adjust to the new order of things in the South? Would the ex-slaves obtain full legal rights? To what degree would blacks participate in politics? How would the former slaves earn a living? How would they interact with their former masters? And what role would the U.S. government play in hammering out answers to these questions?

Reconstruction (1865–1877) was the complex period of readjustment following the Civil War. Reconstruction touched all Americans—blacks and whites, northerners and southerners, and residents of urban and rural communities. It was a period of phenomenal national economic expansion and self-examination. Events during Reconstruction not only reunited the nation, but also redefined the status of the ex-slaves. Most important, Reconstruction altered the basic fabric of American politics. After two centuries of being excluded from the decision-making process, black Americans during Reconstruction became active participants in politics—as voters, elected officials, and political party leaders. Blacks also accomplished other things during Reconstruction. They worked hard to reunite their families, to acquire land, and to educate themselves. Overcoming two hundred years of slavery posed major barriers for the freedpeople. Though many succeeded, it was always an uphill struggle.

The freedpeople received little support from Andrew Johnson, a former Tennessee slaveholder and Democrat, who became president in April 1865, after Abraham Lincoln's assassination. Lincoln, a Republican who initiated freeing the slaves and arming blacks, added Johnson to his 1864 reelection campaign as vice president. Johnson was a strong Unionist who represented poor whites against the planter class. As president, not surprisingly, he sympathized more with whites than with blacks.

Johnson led the country during Reconstruction's first phase: "Presidential Reconstruction," 1865–1867. Determined to reunite the country quickly, during these years he imposed mild terms on the defeated southern states. Johnson believed that rich planters, not yeomen farmers, had caused the war and that only a handful of secessionists should be punished. Encouraged by Johnson's leniency, white southerners reluctantly recognized the blacks' freedom but granted them few legal rights or social privileges. To control them, whites passed Black Codes in 1865–1866, laws that sought to keep blacks in a status as similar to slavery as possible.

Outraged by the unwillingness of white southerners to treat the freedpeople fairly or accept Union control, Johnson's northern Republican opponents in Congress went to work to defeat his program. "Radical" Republicans Charles Sumner, Thaddeus Stevens, Benjamin F. Wade, and others ushered in a second phase: "Congressional Reconstruction," 1867–1877, which lasted through the two administrations of Johnson's successor, President Ulysses S. Grant. Unlike Johnson, the Radicals expected white southerners to accept responsibility for causing the war and to treat their former slaves fairly. During Reconstruction, Radicals led moves in the U.S. Congress to amend the Constitution not only to outlaw slavery but also to define blacks as citizens and to grant them the vote. As Johnson proved unwilling to guarantee black rights, Radicals in Congress took control of Reconstruction from him. Working openly and aggressively against Johnson, the Radicals' civil-rights legislation was in place by 1870, and the Union was virtually restored. Acceptance of the principles of Congressional Reconstruction by the former Confederate states ultimately became the prerequisite for their readmission to the Union.

Given the refusal of white southerners to treat the blacks fairly, Radicals in Congress reasoned that the federal government had to enforce equal political rights and guarantee racial justice. As a result, Congress in 1866 passed a civil-rights act (over Johnson's veto) that conferred basic civil rights on the ex-slaves. In the same year, Congress, again over Johnson's veto, strengthened the Freedmen's Bureau, a federal agency established in 1865 to assist blacks in their adjustment to freedom. The Freedmen's Bureau provided humanitarian aid, established schools, and arbitrated labor contracts between black workers and white landowners.

In 1867–1868, Congress passed a series of Reconstruction Acts that took control of Reconstruction away from Johnson. This legislation placed the former Confederate States under military rule and required them to hold state constitutional conventions and redraft basic laws. Whereas a small but influential portion of white males were prevented from voting because of their previous support of the Confederacy, black men gained an opportunity to vote for the first time and they helped draft new state constitutions that guaranteed universal male suffrage. These revised state constitutions, along with the Fourteenth and Fifteenth Amendments, were among the foremost accomplishments of Congressional Reconstruction. The Fourteenth Amendment, ratified in 1868, guaranteed blacks the rights of citizenship including equal protection before the law. The Fifteenth Amendment, ratified in 1870, gave them the right to vote. At long last, these amendments guaranteed equality of treatment and opportunity. They did so on paper at least.

THE THIRTEENTH AMENDMENT, ratified in 1865

Section 1: Neither slavery nor involuntary servitude, except as a punishment for crime whereof the party shall have been duly convicted, shall exist within the United States, or any place subject to their jurisdiction.

Section 2: Congress shall have power to enforce this article by appropriate legislation.

THE FOURTEENTH AMENDMENT, ratified in 1868

Section 1: All persons born or naturalized in the United States, and subject to the jurisdiction thereof, are citizens of the United States and of the State wherein they reside. No State shall make or enforce any law which shall abridge the privileges or immunities of citizens of the United States; nor shall any State deprive any person of life, liberty, or property, without due process of law; nor deny to any person within its jurisdiction the equal protection of the laws.

Section 2: Representatives shall be apportioned among the several States according to their respective numbers, counting the whole number of persons in each State, excluding Indians not taxed. But when the right to vote at any election for the choice of electors for President and Vice President of the United States, Representatives in Congress, the Executive and Judicial officers of a State, or the members of the Legislature thereof, is denied to any of the male inhabitants of such State, being twenty-one years of age, and citizens of the United States, or in any way abridged, except for participation in rebellion, or other crime, the basis of representation therein shall be reduced in the proportion which the number of such male citizens shall bear to the whole number of male citizens twenty-one years of age in such State.

Section 3: No person shall be a Senator or Representative in Congress, or elector of President and Vice President, or hold any office, civil or military, under the United States, or under any State, who, having previously taken an oath, as a member of Congress, or as an officer of the United States, or as a member of any State legislature, or as an executive or judicial officer of any State, to support the Constitution of the United States, shall have engaged in insurrection or rebellion against the same, or given aid or comfort to the enemies thereof. But Congress may by a vote of two-thirds of each House, remove such disability.

Section 4: The validity of the public debt of the United States, authorized by law, including debts incurred for payment of pensions and bounties of services in suppressing insurrection or rebellion, shall not be questioned. But neither the United States nor any State shall assume or pay any debt or obligation incurred in aid of insurrection or rebellion against the United States, or any claim for the loss or emancipation of any slave; but all such debts, obligations and claims shall be held illegal and void.

Section 5: The Congress shall have power to enforce, by appropriate legislation, the provisions of this article.

THE FIFTEENTH AMENDMENT, ratified in 1870

Section 1: The right of citizens of the United States to vote shall not be denied or abridged by the United States or by any State on account of race, color, or previous condition of servitude.

Section 2: The Congress shall have power to enforce this article by appropriate legislation.

During Reconstruction the former slaves, now freedmen and women, set a new agenda. They asserted themselves in every part of their lives. When the war concluded, the freedpeople reassembled their families, which had been separated by slavery. They tested their freedom by settling on abandoned lands, by moving from farms and plantations to towns and cities, by challenging their former masters' economic control, and by establishing separate black churches. The freedmen and women were determined to collect "forty acres and a mule" as compensation for their years of toil as slaves. This phrase resulted from General William T. Sherman's January 1865, "Special Field Order No. 15" that reserved 40-acre farms for the freedpeople under Sherman's jurisdiction. The general agreed to lend the ex-slaves horses and mules as well.

Resolved to make a living on their own land, the blacks drew heavily on agricultural and marketing skills they had developed as slaves. The blacks also established schools, churches, and banks throughout the former Confederacy. Under Congressional Reconstruction, the freedmen organized politically, joining the Republican party and supporting its candidates throughout the South. In short, they worked doggedly to become economically and socially independent and established political clout in their states and in national affairs.

~~~~~

This book captures the voices of blacks—men and women, farmers and politicians, illiterate and educated—caught in the throes of Reconstruction. Their words provide a rich documentary record of the hopes and dreams, struggles and frustrations, of blacks as they sought to break the chains of slavery and its long legacy. The book contains various letters, newspaper articles, congressional testimony, and other comments by blacks who sensed the importance of Reconstruction as the defining moment for their future. After examining thousands of documents, I have included representative samples that recount the history of Reconstruction from the black perspective. I have reproduced the blacks' writings exactly as I found them, retaining the original spelling, grammar, capitalization, and most punctuation. These texts include such outdated terms as "colored" and "Negro"— even the offensive word "nigger." These materials convey the tone, tenor, and flavor of the times when the freedpeople lived. Many of the writers were illiterate, unlearned, and impoverished, but not unintelligent. They had an intimate understanding of the world around them and what they wanted for themselves and their families—freedom, economic security, and better futures for their children. My goal was to chart the early struggles, the optimism and, later, the disappointment of a people caught in the midst of dramatic social, political, and economic change.

Chronology

1862 April 16: Emancipation of slaves in the District of Columbia

July 22: Discussion of Emancipation Proclamation in Lincoln's cabinet

September 22: Lincoln issues Preliminary Emancipation Proclamation

1863 January 1: Lincoln issues Emancipation Proclamation

June 20: West Virginia adopts constitution providing for gradual emancipation

1864 October 29: Maryland constitution abolishing slavery in effect

1865 January 11: Emancipation in Missouri in effect

January 31: Thirteenth Amendment passed

February 22: Emancipation in Tennessee in effect

March 3: Freedmen's Bureau established

April 9: Robert E. Lee surrenders to U. S. Grant

May 29: President Andrew Johnson announces Reconstruction plans

June 13: Johnson appoints provisional governors for six former Confederate states

November 24: Mississippi passes its Black Code

December 13: Joint Committee of Fifteen on Reconstruction established

December 18: Thirteenth Amendment ratified

December 24: Ku Klux Klan formed in Tennessee

1866 February 19: Freedmen's Bureau extended and expanded

April 9: Civil Rights Act passed over Johnson's veto

May 1: Memphis race riot

June 16: Fourteenth Amendment passed

July 16: Freedmen's Bureau legislation passed over Johnson's veto

July 30: New Orleans race riot

1867 March 2: First Reconstruction Act passed over Johnson's veto

March 22: Second Reconstruction Act passed over Johnson's veto

July 19: Third Reconstruction Act passed over Johnson's veto

1868 March 11: Fourth Reconstruction Act passed

July 20: Fourteenth Amendment ratified

1869 February 27: Fifteenth Amendment passed

1870 May 31: First Enforcement Act passed

1871 April 20: Third Enforcement (Ku Klux Klan) Act passed

1872 June 10: Freedmen's Bureau abolished

1875 March 1: Civil Rights Act passed

1877 April 24: Last U.S. Army troops withdrawn from the South

1883 October 15: U.S. Supreme Court declares Civil Rights Act of 1875 unconstitutional

Black Voices
from Reconstruction

Chapter One

THE PROMISE AND REALITY OF EMANCIPATION

"It is my Desire to be free."

In many ways the processes of emancipation and Reconstruction went hand in hand during the Civil War. As Union troops entered the South in 1861, they encountered slaves, many of whom jumped at the opportunity to leave their masters and work for their liberators, the northern invaders. Early in the war President Abraham Lincoln explained repeatedly that the conflict was being fought to keep the Union intact, not to free the slaves. But for the South's black slaves, the war meant the opportunity to be free. Slaves on St. Helena Island, South Carolina, for example, became free as early as November 1861, when the U.S. Army captured the coastal Sea Islands.

By late 1862, Lincoln changed his mind regarding the North's war aims. In September he issued the Preliminary Emancipation Proclamation, hopeful that the South would surrender without having to emancipate its slaves. In this proclamation, Lincoln warned that if Confederate soldiers did not lay down their arms by January 1, 1863, all slaves then in Confederate territory would be freed. Significantly, the Emancipation Proclamation did not apply to slaves held in Union territory. The South's failure to heed Lincoln's call led not only to the start of wartime emancipation, but also to the beginning of Reconstruction.

Discovering Freedom

 Emancipation was a complex process, differing from state to state, county to county, and individual case to individual case. Slaves learned about their freedom in various ways and responded accordingly. Many years after emancipation North Carolina's Sara Debro recalled that "When de War was over de Yankees was all around de place, tellin' de niggers what to do. Dey told dem dey was free, dat dey didn't have to slave for de white folks no more."[1] Though diverse in their actions, the ex-slaves agreed that emancipation was a gift from God.

Annie Davis, a slave in Belair, Maryland, wrote President Lincoln in August 1864, inquiring into her legal status. Maryland was a loyal slave state that did not outlaw slavery until November 1864. Impatient for her freedom, Annie wanted to find members of her family who had been traded away as slaves on Maryland's Eastern Shore, but her master would not allow her to leave. "It is my Desire to be free," Annie wrote Lincoln. "You will please let me know if we are free," she instructed the President, "and what i can do. I write to you for advice." The slave asked Lincoln to "please send me word this week. or as soon as possible and oblidge."[2]

Willis, a former slave from Burke County, Georgia, recalled his moment of emancipation:

> When freedom was declared, I went down to Augusta to
> de Freedman's Bureau to see if 'twas true, we was free. . . .
> De man got up and stated to de people: "You all is just as
> free as I am. You ain't got no mistis and no marster. Work
> when you want." On Sunday morning Old Marster . . . tell
> us to all come to do house. He said: "What I want to see
> for you all is to tell you dat you are free. You have de
> privilege to go anywhere you want, but I don't want none
> o'you to leave me now. I wants you-all to stay right with
> me. If you stay, you must sign to it."

Unlike the other newly freed blacks, Willis refused to sign the agreement. He informed his former master: "If I is already free, I don't need to sign no paper. It I was workin' for you and doin for you before I got free, I can do it still, if you wants me to stay with you." Ultimately Willis decided to stay with his ex-master, now his employer. He received rations plus fifteen dollars a month as pay.[3]

Ezra Adams, who described himself as "a right smart size plow boy, when freedom come" on his master's plantation in Lancaster County, South Carolina, recalled how tentative, how uncertain the slaves were of the meaning of emancipation. Reflecting on when he was freed, Adams said:

> You ain't gwine to believe dat de slaves on our plantation
> didn't stop workin' for old marster, even when they was
> told dat they was free. Us didn't want no more freedom
> than us was gittin' on our plantation already. Us knowed
> too well dat us was well took care of, wid a plenty of vittles
> to eat and tight log and board houses to live in. De slaves,
> where I lived, knowed after de war dat they had abun-
> dance of dat somethin' called freedom, what they could
> not [e]at, wear, and sleep in. . . . Dis livin' on liberty is lak
> young folks livin' on love after they gits married. It just

don't work. No, sir, it las' so long and not a bit longer....
It sho' don't hold good when you has to work, or when
you gits hongry.

After Adams had acquired his own land, however, he changed his tune. "If a poor man wants to enjoy a little freedom," he said, "let him go on de farm and work for hisself. It is sho' worth somethin' to be boss, and, on de farm you can be boss all you want to."[4]

Early in 1865 twenty ex-slaves, ministers, and prominent community leaders gathered in Savannah, Georgia, to meet Secretary of War Edwin M. Stanton and General William T. Sherman. They discussed what slavery and the Emancipation Proclamation meant to them and what they wanted for the future. The New York *Daily Tribune* reported the interview between the white officials and the black leaders. According to their spokesman, sixty-seven-year-old Baptist preacher Garrison Frazier, blacks believed that

slavery is, receiving by irresistible power the work of another man, and not by his consent. The freedom, as I understand it, promised by the proclamation, is taking us from under the yoke of bondage, and placing us where we could reap the fruit of our own labor, take care of ourselves and assist the Government in maintaining our freedom.

Frazier went on to say:

The way we can best take care of ourselves is to have land, and turn it and till it by our own labor ... and we can soon maintain ourselves and have something to spare. And to assist the Government, the young men should enlist in the service of the Government, and serve in such manner as they may be wanted.... We want to be placed on land until we are able to buy it and make it our own.[5]

Thousands of other slaves, called "contraband" (a term for runaway Confederate slaves coined by Union General Benjamin F. Butler in 1861), received their freedom by fleeing their masters and entering Union army camps. Some of the newly freed men enlisted in the U.S. Colored Troops to fight their former masters. Others, including freedwomen and children, performed various tasks for the army—as cooks, servants, spies, guides, teamsters, draymen (men who drove carts), coopers (barrel makers), blacksmiths, pioneers (men who cleared forests), fortification laborers, and railroad workers. Those who accompanied the federal armies on the march saw a world beyond their former plantations and farms. But the freedpeople quickly discovered that the Union Army often treated them only slightly less harshly than their former masters.

A case in point is that of four ex-slaves—Anna and Laura Irwin, Rhoda Willis, and Milly Humphries who served as washerwomen for the U.S. Army General Field Hospital, Department of the Cumberland, Tennessee. From 1864 until 1865 these women worked for the army in Georgia, Tennessee, and Alabama. After the war, however, they complained to the Freedmen's Bureau that the army owed them wages. The women found that collecting their pay in a free-market economy was more difficult than they had supposed.

Other former slaves complained that during their government service they actually lost property accumulated while enslaved. Masters commonly allowed slaves to raise crops such as vegetables, to fish, and to hunt for their own use and for sale to whites in their locality. Many slaves also raised livestock. They acquired property either by paying cash or by bartering goods. Coastal slaves who cropped rice on the "task system" often completed their work assignments early and then had the remainder of the day to labor for themselves. Accumulation of private property obviously was a special and meaningful activity for a people who, under the various state slave codes, were not entitled to own even their own bodies. Ironically, however, upon emancipation many ex-slaves lost property and privileges they had painstakingly acquired in bondage.

After the war, for example, Nancy Johnson, a former slave from Liberty County, Georgia, told a federal commission that the Union soldiers who freed her and her husband also stripped them of the means of providing for themselves. As a slave, Nancy informed the officials, her husband "did his tasks & after that he worked for himself." "He worked Sundays too," she added, "and that was for ourselves. . . . He always was a hardworking man." Nancy's husband eventually earned enough money to purchase chickens, horses, and hogs.

In the following testimony, Nancy recounts the rigors of life in the throes of emancipation and the struggles the freedpeople experienced as they gained their freedom. First she describes the harsh conditions of slave labor during the war along Canoochie Creek in Confederate Georgia.

I was served mighty mean before the Yankees came here. I was nearly frostbitten: my old Missus made me weave to make clothes for the [Confederate] soldiers till 12 o'clock at night & I was so tired. . . . I had to work hard for the rebels until the very last day when they took us. The old man [Nancy's former master] came to me then & said if you won't go away & will work for us we will work for you; I told him if the other colored people were going to be free that I wanted to be [too]. I went away & then came back & my old Missus asked me if I came back to behave myself & do her work . . . I told her no[,] that I came to do my own work. I went to my own house & in the morning my old master came to me & asked me if I wouldn't go and milk the cows: I told him that my Missus had driven me off . . . then my Mistress . . . asked me if I came back to work for her like a "*nigger*"—I told her no that I was free & she said be off then & called me a stinking bitch. . . . I have been hard up to live but thank God, I am spared yet. I quit then [and] only did a few jobs for her but she never did anything for me except give me a meal of victuals. . . . I was hard up then, I was well to do before the war.

At first the Johnsons welcomed the Union troops who entered Georgia as liberators. Nancy described her husband as "a good Union man" who once harbored an escaped Union soldier in their slave cabin before helping him make his way to safety. In terms of their loyalty to the Union, Nancy said, "His heart was right & so was mine." But they soon came to hate the Yankees.

The change occurred when Union troops swept through Liberty County, randomly and openly seizing property—both that of masters and slaves—in their path. They stole most of the Johnsons' hard-earned possessions. Nancy explained:

I had tried to hide things. They found our meat, it was hid under the house & they took a crop of rice. They took it out & I had some cloth under the house too & the dishes & two fine bed-quilts. . . . These were all my own labor & night labor. They took the bole of cloth under the house and the next morning they came back with it made into pantaloons. They were starved & naked almost. . . . They took all my husbands clothes, except what he had on his back.

They took the mare out of the stable; they took the bacon under the house, the corn was taken out of the crib, & the rice & the lard. Some of the chickens they shot & some they run down; they shot the hogs.

(?)SLAVERY
CIVIL RIGHTS

EMANCIPA
PROCLAMATIO
JANUARY 1ST
1863.

ALL PERSONS
HELD AS SLAVES
WITHIN ANY STATES
UNITED STATES
SHALL BE THEN
THENCE FORWARD
AND FOREVER
FREE
A. LINCOLN.
SEWARD

SLAVERY
IS
ABOLISHED
BY THE
STATES AND U.S.
CONGRESS

STATE RIG

THE
LAND OF THE
FREE.

Negroes Sold as a Punishment for Crime.

"PUBLIC SALE.—The undersigned will offer for sale, at the Court-house door in the City of Annapolis, at 11 o'clock A.M., on Saturday, the 22d of December, a negro man named Jno. Johnson, aged about 40 years. The said negro was convicted at the October term, 1866, of the Circuit Court of Ann Arundel County, of larceny, and sentenced to be sold.   WM. BRYAN, *Sheriff.*"

"BALTIMORE, DEC 24.—Four negroes convicted of larceny, and ordered to be sold by Judge Magruder, at Annapolis, were sold on Saturday last."

'8

This print by American illustrator Thomas Nast comments on the abuses that persisted in the South even after slavery was declared illegal.

> I told one of the officers that we would starve & they said no that we would get it all back again, ... The Lord forgive them for the way they have treated me.

All in all, according to Nancy, the Union soldiers stole from the Johnsons between thirty and forty chickens, eleven hogs, four or five bushels of corn meal, and one-half a barrel of lard, tubs, kettles, and a silk dress belonging to one of her daughters. Shocked by the entire experience, Nancy wrote that she had never imagined that "a Yankee person would be so mean." Though her husband submitted a claim for $514.50 to the U.S. government for the property seized by Union soldiers, it eventually awarded him less than one-half, only $155.[6]

Another former slave, Samuel Larkin of Hunstville, Alabama, had more success in securing compensation from a postwar federal commission. During the war Samuel served as a laborer with a Union regiment and accumulated about $500, which he invested in horses and mules. Industrious and disciplined, he established his own transport/express business in Nashville and profited from the booming wartime economy. In August 1863, however, a squad of Union soldiers confiscated Samuel's animals, wagons, equipment, and supplies. Larkin was one of the more successful claimants. Nine years later his claim against the government for $400 finally was settled. He received $350.[7]

North Carolina freedmen had their own complaints concerning treatment by the federal government. Shortly before the end of the war, blacks living in a contraband camp on Roanoke Island, North Carolina, met to air a variety of grievances, including actions taken by the camp's white administrators, superintendent Horace James and his assistant Holland Streeter. The blacks, who served as government teamsters and fortification laborers, sent several petitions to President Lincoln and Secretary of War Edwin M. Stanton seeking improved treatment.

The recently emancipated men wanted to know what their rights were. They explained:

> We dont exspect to have the same wrights as white men doe we know that [we] are in a millitary country and we exspect to obey the rules and orders of our authories and doe as they say doe, any thing in reason we thanks God and thank our President for all of his aids for what has been done for us but are not satisfide with our Supertendent nor the treatment we receives. . . .

The men felt opresssed by James and Streeter, the very people they looked to for help. In the petition the freedmen wrote that they felt "entily friendless." They charged that the U.S. Army "treated us [as] mean [as] . . . our owners ever did . . . just like we had been dum beast." White soldiers abused them verbally and scared them with firecrackers.

Specifically, the black North Carolinians complained that James broke his word. He had promised them easy access to building materials but then dishonestly placed obstacles in their way to obtain wood planks with which to build houses. In addition, the freedmen asserted that the superintendent rarely paid the monthly $10 promised them for their labor. Some men who worked on fortifications allegedly had not been paid in three years. The ex-slaves also charged that it was impossible to satisfy the superintendent. James frequently encouraged them to work independently, but then penalized the blacks for doing so. The petitioners explained:

> Soon as he Sees we are trying to Support our Selves without the aid of the Government he comes and make a Call for the men, that is not working for the Government to Goe away and if we are not willing to Goe he orders the Guards to take us by the point of the bayonet, and we have no power to help it we know it is wright and are willing

to doe any thing that the President or our head Command-
ers want us to doe but we are not willing to be pull and
haul a bout so much . . . as we have been for the last two
years and we may say Get nothing for it. . . .

Despite their complaints, the petitioners informed Lincoln of
their loyalty and determination to serve the government. But, they
added, U.S. authorities were treating them inhumanely and
allowing their families to starve. As one petition proclaimed:

We are not willing to work as we have done . . . and be
Troden under foot and Get nothing for it we have work
faithful Since we have been on the Island we have built
our log houses we have Cultivate our acre of Ground and
have Tried to be less exspence to the Government as we
Possible Could be and we are yet Trying to help the Government all we Can. . . . those head men have done every
thing to us that our masters have done except by and Sell
us and now they are Trying to Starve the woman & children to death cutting off they ration . . . now . . . they wont
Give them no meat to eat, every ration day beef & a little
fish and . . . they are going from one to another Trying to
borrow a little meal to last until ration day.

The freedmen also alleged that James and Streeter forced
their young sons, against their parents' wishes, to labor for the
army in Newbern, North Carolina.

[They] Send them to newbern to work to pay for they ration without they parent Consint . . . we thought was very
hard that . . . our boy Children . . . Goe to School hard as
times are, but rather then they Should Goe without learning we thought we would try and doe it and say no more
about it . . . the first thing we knowed Mr Stereeter . . . had

Gone a round to all the White School-Teachers and told them to Give the boys orders to goe and get they ration on a Cirtain day. . . . So Some twenty or twenty-five went and Mr Streeter Give them they rations and the Guard march them down to the head quarters and put them on board the boat and carried them to newbern here is woman . . . on the Island which their husbands are in the army just had one little boy to help them to cut & lug wood & to Goe arrand for them. . . . James has taken them and sent them away Some of these little ones . . . wasen oer 12 years olds. the mothers of Some went . . . and Grieved and beg for the little boys but he [James] would not let them have them we want to know if the Prisident done essued any ration for School boys if he dont then we are satisfide we have men on the Island that Can Support the boys to Goe to School but here are Poor woman [who] are not able to do it So the orphans must Goe without they learning that all we can say a bout the matter.

In their petitions, the former slaves on Roanoke Island argued that the U.S. government officials treated them so poorly "because they think that we are igorant." Disappointed with their circumstances, the blacks found dealing with the government far more difficult than they had expected. They had to negotiate with bureaucrats for the basics of life, including food and housing. In one of their petitions the blacks concluded that "all we wants is a Chance and we can Get a living like White men." Unfortunately, despite their impassioned pleas, the government never addressed the petitioners' complaints.[8]

Redefining Freedom

General Robert E. Lee's surrender in April 1865 signaled not only the end of the war but, for all practical purposes, slavery as well.

Inspired by Confederate defeat, blacks throughout the South began defining the meaning of freedom for themselves and constructing what historian Elsa Barkley Brown has termed "communities of struggle." They assembled in mass meetings, determined their goals, outlined their concerns, and charted new lives as freedmen and women. The former slaves stood determined to claim and secure freedom as broadly as possible.

For example, on June 10, 1865, more than 3,000 freedpeople crowded into Richmond, Virginia's, First African Baptist Church to hear a "protest memorial" sent on their behalf to President Andrew Johnson. "Mr. President," they wrote, "We have been appointed a committee by a public meeting of the colored people of Richmond, Va., to make known . . . the wrongs, as we conceive them to be, by which we are sorely oppressed." They objected to regulations that limited their mobility, their attempts to reunite their families, to work where and for whom they wanted, and to protect their homes and personal property against seizure.

Richmond's blacks, however, emphasized more than just the harsh treatment they received at the hands of whites. They stressed their readiness for full citizenship. They explained:

> We represent a population of more than 20,000 colored people, including Richmond and Manchester, . . . more than 6,000 of our people are members . . . of Christian churches, and nearly our whole population . . . attend divine services. Among us there are at least 2,000 men who are worth $200 to $500; 200 who have property valued at from $1,000 to $5,000, and a number who are worth from $5,000 to $20,000.

The freedpeople went on to point out their accomplishments under slavery. They noted that "the law of slavery severely punished those who taught us to read and write, but, not withstanding this,

3,000 of us can read, and at least 2,000 can read and write, and a large number of us are engaged in useful and profitable employment on our own account." And, in spite of slavery, they said,

> None of our people are in the alms-house, and when we were slaves the aged and infirm who were turned away from the homes of hard masters, who had been enriched by their toil, our benevolent societies supported while they lived, and buried when they died, and comparatively few of us have found it necessary to ask for Government rations, which have been so bountifully bestowed upon the unrepentant Rebels of Richmond. . . . During the . . . Slaveholders' Rebellion we have been true and loyal to the United States Government; . . . We have given aid and comfort to the soldiers of freedom (for which several of our people, of both sexes, have been severely punished by stripes and imprisonment). We have been their pilots and their scouts, and have safely conducted them through many perilous adventures.

Despite their ordeal, then, Richmond's freedmen and women remained optimistic and loyal to the U.S. government. In addition to observing such traditional patriotic holidays as Washington's Birthday and Independence Day, on April 3 they celebrated their special day—Emancipation Day.[9]

T 39179

Chapter Two

CHANGING OLD WAYS

"... We are defenceless before our enemies."

Black southerners made every effort to establish themselves as a community of freedpeople during and after the Civil War. To do so, they first had to free themselves from the clutches of the slaveholders, their former owners. Once they had shed the conditions of slavery imposed by their former masters, they could assert themselves as never before. Rarely, however, was this an easy task.

Throughout Reconstruction former masters sought to maintain control over their ex-slaves. Two centuries of owning and controlling their black laborers convinced them that men and women of African heritage were inferior and that their agricultural and social systems depended on slavery. Threatened by what they viewed as revolutionary change, whites sought to keep blacks in a condition as close to slavery as possible. In Orange County, North Carolina, Sara Debro's former master made her leave her comfortable slave cabin, forcing Sara to live in housing built by Union soldiers. These, she complained, resembled "poor white folks' houses, little shacks made out of sticks and mud with sticks and mud chimneys."[1]

Attempts at Reenslavement

Few white southerners accepted the idea of emancipation easily or painlessly. Many never accepted it at all. Not surprisingly, former slaves worried that their former masters would try to reenslave them. According to a leading black newspaper, the Washington *New Era,* "The freedmen at first quite largely distrusted their former owners, and feared . . . that unless they fled the scene of their servitude, they should be again enslaved."[2]

The freedpeople had good reason to harbor such fears. In 1865, for example, Alabama's new legislature adopted the Thirteenth Amendment but added an amendment of its own restricting the role of the U.S. Congress in defining the status of its black citizens. White Alabamians would accept emancipation, the legislators said, but were unwilling to "confer upon Congress the power to legislate upon the political status of freedmen in this state."[3]

A year later former slave Richard R. Hill of Hampton, Virginia, informed a congressional committee that whites were committed to returning the freedmen to a status "little better than that of the slaves" by passing laws that kept the former bondsmen and women in a separate and unequal status.[4]

According to one black observer, white southerners remained bitter and resentful long after the loss of their slaves. They never would accept the reality of emancipation. "Nothing," he added, "will ever heal the wound which this great wrong has done them, and fully reconcile them to the Government of the Union. . . ."[5]

In many cases masters failed to inform the slaves of their freedom, tricked them into some form of quasi-slavery, or forced the former slaves from their land to fend for themselves. Henry Adams, who lived twenty-two years as a slave near Shreveport, Louisiana, recalled his first months of freedom in 1865:

After they told us we were free—even then they would not let us live as man and wife together. And when we would run away to be free from slavery, the white people would not let us come on their places to see our mothers, wives, sisters, or fathers. We was made to leave the place, or made to go back and live as slaves.... there was over two thousand colored people killed trying to get away, after the white people told us we were free.... Many of the colored people were killed, but the white people pretended to know little about it. I seen some shot dead because they left with a white woman.[6]

Blacks in Virginia told a similar, unfortunate story. In June 1865—two months after the war's end—they complained that whites continued to treat them like slaves. Former Confederates returned "with all their old pride and contempt for the negro transformed into bitter hate for the new-made freeman." In Richmond, hundreds of freedpeople were arrested simply because they walked the streets without a "pass." In rural areas white planters agreed not to hire any blacks except their own former slaves or others "without a written recommendation from their late employers." They threatened to use force against those who ignored such warnings, "thereby," according to a delegation of Norfolk blacks, "keeping us in a state of serfdom, and preventing our free selection of our employers...." The Norfolk blacks added:

In many of the more remote districts, individual planters are to be found who still refuse to recognize their negroes as free, forcibly retaining the wives and children of their late escaped slaves; cases have occurred not far from Richmond itself, in which an attempt to leave the plantation has been punished by shooting to death; and finally, there are a number of cases known to ourselves in the immediate vicinity in which a faithfull performance, by colored men, of the duties of labor contracted for, has been met by a contemptuous and violent refusal of the stipulated compensation.[7]

The case of former slave Jourdon Anderson suggests just how cautious the freedpeople had to be in their dealings with those who had once owned them. Jourdon's Tennessee master, Colonel P. H. Anderson, attempted to shoot him as he fled from slavery. In 1865, Colonel Anderson wrote Jourdon, asking him to return to work for him as a free laborer. Writing Anderson from the safe confines of Dayton, Ohio, the highly literate ex-slave explained that he and his wife were suspicious of their former master's intentions. Informing the colonel of his concerns, Jourdon wrote:

As to my freedom, which you say I can have, there is nothing to be gained on that score, as I got my free-papers in 1864 from the Provost-Marshal-General of the Department at Nashville. Mandy says she would be afraid to go back without some proof that you are sincerely disposed to treat us fairly and justly—and we have concluded to test your sincerity by asking you to send us our wages for the time we served you. This will make us forget and forgive old scores, and rely on your justice and friendship in the future. I served you faithfully for thirty-two years and Mandy twenty years. At $25 a month for me, and $2 a week for Mandy, our earnings would amount to $11,680. Add to this the interest for the time of our wages has been kept and deduct what you paid for our clothing and three doctors visits to me, and pulling a tooth for Mandy, and the balance will show what we are in justice entitled to.... If you fail to pay us for faithful labors in the past we can have little faith in your promises in the future. We trust the good Maker has opened your eyes to the wrongs which

> you and your fathers have done to me and my fathers, in
> making us toil for generations without recompense. Here
> I draw my wages every Saturday night, but in Tennessee
> there was never any pay day for the negroes any more
> than for the horses and cows. Surely there will be a day of
> reckoning for those who defraud the laborer of his hire.

After signing his letter, Jourdon added: "P.S.—Say howdy to George Carter, and thank him for taking the pistol from you when you were shooting at me."[8]

The Black Codes: Conditional Freedom

 The fears of Jourdon and other former slaves were justified. Determined to reconstruct the Union as quickly as possible, President Johnson in 1865 generously allowed most whites, including former Confederate officials, to vote when reestablishing their state governments. The freedpeople, however, could not vote. The president required the southern states to recognize in their laws that blacks were free. But that, however, was as far as he was willing to go.

With few restrictions imposed by the federal government, not surprisingly in 1865 white southerners elected former Confederates and ex-slaveholders to lead their new state governments. While southern state legislators reluctantly repealed their old slave laws, they replaced them with new laws designed to control the freedpeople: the Black Codes.

These laws allowed the freedmen and women to own property, to marry, and to bring cases to court. But they imposed severe limitations on their freedom. Across the South, blacks—including women and children—were required to work. Unemployed black adults were liable to be sentenced to labor without pay for whites. Unemployed black children were to be apprenticed to whites.

Mississippi's Black Code, for example, restricted where blacks could purchase or rent land. It also included a catch-all section that punished blacks who were convicted of

> committing riots, routs, affrays, trespasses, malicious mischief, cruel treatment to animals, seditious speeches, insulting gestures, language, or acts, or assaults on any person, disturbance of the peace, exercising the function of a minister of the Gospel without a license . . . vending spirituous or intoxicating liquors, or committing any other misdemeanor. . . .[9]

South Carolina's Black Code required blacks to purchase an expensive license in order to work at certain jobs. While freedpeople there could testify in trials involving other blacks, they were not allowed to sit on juries or join the state militia. The state's Black Code defined vagrancy broadly, including "those who are engaged in representing publicly or privately, for fee or reward, without license, any tragedy, interlude, comedy, farce, play, or other similar entertainment, exhibition of the circus, sleight-of-hand, wax-works, or the like." The masters of a black apprentice were permitted "to inflict moderate chastisement and impose reasonable restraint . . . and to recapture him if he depart from his service."[10]

Outraged by their state's Black Code, in November 1865, South Carolina freedmen met in Charleston and organized a Colored People's Convention. According to the delegates, "In our humble opinion, a code of laws for the government of *all,* regardless of color, is all that is necessary for the advancement of the interests and prosperity of the State." In their proceedings the blacks informed white South Carolinians:

RE-CONSTRUCTION,
OR "A WHITE MAN'S GOVERNMENT".

Heretofore we have had no avenues opened to us or our children—we have had no firesides that we could call our own; none of those incentives to work for the development of our minds and the aggrandizement of our race in common with other people. The measures which have been adopted for the development of white men's children have been denied to us and ours. The laws which have made white men great, have degraded us, because we were colored, and because we were reduced to chattel slavery. But now that we are freemen, now that we have been lifted up by the providence of God to manhood, we have resolved to come forward, and, like MEN, speak and *act* for ourselves. . . .

Thus we would address you, not as enemies, but as friends and fellow-countrymen, who desire to dwell among you in peace, and whose destinies are interwoven, and linked with those of the American people, and hence must be fulfilled in this country. As descendants of a race feeble and long oppressed, we might . . . appeal to a great and magnanimous people like Americans, for special favors and encouragement, on the principle that the strong aid the weak, the learned should teach the unlearned. . . .

We ask for no special privileges or peculiar favors. We ask only for *even-handed Justice,* or for the removal of such . . . obstructions and disabilities as . . . Legislators have seen fit to throw in our way, and heap upon us. . . .

We simply desire that we shall be recognized as men; that we have no obstructions placed in our way; that the same laws which govern white men shall direct colored men; that we have the right of trial by a jury of our peers, that schools be opened or established for our children; that we be permitted to acquire homesteads for ourselves and children; that we be dealt with . . . in equity and justice.[11]

Disappointed with the limitations on their new freedom, blacks throughout the South organized and protested. From Norfolk, Virginia, came a petition that summarized the problems the freedpeople experienced. According to black leaders, including Joseph T. Wilson and H. Highland Garnet,

we have no means of legally making or enforcing contracts of any description; we have no right to testify before the courts in any case in which a white man is one of the parties to the suits; we are taxed without representation; and, in short, so far as legal safeguards of our rights are concerned, we are defenceless before our enemies.

We are still more unfortunately situated as regards our late masters. They have returned to their homes, with all their old pride and contempt for the negro transformed into bitter hate for the new-made freeman. . . . in the greater number of counties in this State meetings have been held, at which resolutions have been adopted, *deploring* while accepting the abolition of slavery, but going on to pledge the planters composing the meeting to employ no negroes save such as were formerly owned by themselves, without a written recommendation from their late employers, thereby keeping us in a state of serfdom, and preventing our free selection of our employers.[12]

According to these black Virginians, only the vote would empower them to overcome their problems.

The Black Codes were only the first of many indicators that whites would resist the idea of freeing their former slaves fully and fairly. During Presidential Reconstruction many white southerners not only tried to lock the blacks into a kind of neo-slavery but also committed unjust labor practices and many violent acts to keep them in line. Blacks found themselves being treated unfairly even in the courts.

In October 1865, a freedman in Raleigh, North Carolina, informed a northern journalist that in his state the scales of justice always seemed to be tipped in favor of the whites. "When a white man and a nigger gets into the scales," he wrote, "don't I know the nigger is always mighty light." He explained:

Yes, we are ignorant. We know it. I am ignorant . . . and they say all niggers is. They say we don't know what the word constitution means. But if we don't know enough to know what the Constitution is, we know enough to know what justice is. I can see for myself down at my own court-house. If they makes a white man pay five dollars for something to-day, and makes a nigger pay ten dollars for doing that thing tomorrow, don't I know that ain't justice?[13]

Convinced that whites were insincere in their willingness to treat the blacks honestly, the New Orleans *Tribune,* the first black daily newspaper published in the United States, warned readers to be suspicious of whites who tried to convince them that they were their "tried" and true "friends." The editor informed whites:

Now, to keep a man in the hardest bondage, to crush his body by excessive labor and his soul by absolute ignorance, to whip him, to undertake a gigantic war in order to better deprive him of his liberty and shorten his chains, and after that . . . to tell us that you are our TRIED friends, is more than a lie, it is a cruel insult and nothing short of it.

If whites were the blacks' real friends, the editor continued, they would encourage, not discourage, granting them civil and political rights. But, no, he said, whites looked back approvingly to slavery and viewed suspiciously a future built upon the principles of racial democracy. "What friendship is that," the journalist asked, "but the deceiving and false friendship of impostors and hypocrites?"[14]

Chapter Three

REUNITING FAMILIES

"I have feeling as well as white person. . . ."

In addition to proving and understanding their new freedom, during Reconstruction no issue was more important to the former slaves than reassembling their families. Under slavery, masters had separated black families in order to make a profit, sometimes doing so for disciplinary reasons. Children were sold away from their mothers and fathers, husbands and wives were forced to live apart, and many slaves never knew their relatives, including their own parents. Modern scholars emphasize the strength of the slave family as a means that blacks used to withstand the horrors of the "peculiar institution." Oral history—stories and remembrances of kinfolk—enabled them to discover their African and American roots and to link generations of slaves over time. Still, the disruption of their families took a heavy toll on the slaves.

Looking for Lost Relatives

 Once free, the ex-slaves set their sights on locating sons, daughters, mothers, and fathers sold as slaves throughout the South.

The goal of blacks always was the same: reconstructing their families and establishing themselves as free persons. In fact, for many years after freedom blacks submitted "Information Wanted" notices in black newspapers in order to track down relatives who had been separated by sale under slavery.

For example, just as soon as they were emancipated, Willis and his wife, former slaves from Burke County, Georgia, went to Waynesboro, Georgia, so that she could be reunited with her parents. They had been separated by slavery for fifteen years. Throughout the South former slaves were determined to reconnect with their loved ones.

Post-Civil War black newspapers commonly ran advertisements for "lost" family members. In 1865, for example, the Nashville *Colored Tennesseean* published these notices:

> Information Wanted of Caroline Dodson, who was sold from Nashville, Nov. 1st, 1862, by James Lumsden to Warwick (a trader then in human beings), who carried her to Atlanta, Georgia, and she was last heard of in the sale pen of Robert Clarke, (human trader in that place), from which she was sold. Any information of her whereabouts will be thankfully received and rewarded by her mother. Lucinda Lowery, Nashville.

> $200 Reward. During the year 1849, Thomas Sample carried away from this city, as his slaves, our daughter, Polly, and son, Geo. Washington, to the State of Mississippi, and subsequently, to Texas, and when last heard from they were in Lagrange, Texas. We will give $100 each for them to any person who will assist them, or either of them, to get to Nashville, or get word to us of their whereabouts, if they are alive. Ben & Flora East.

> Saml. Dove wishes to know of the whereabouts of his mother, Areno, his sisters Maria, Neziah, and Peggy, and

his brother Edmond, who were owned by Geo. Dove, of Rockingham county, Shenandoah Valley, Va. Sold in Richmond, after which Saml. and Edmond were taken to Nashville, Tenn., by Joe Mick; Areno was left at the Eagle Tavern, Richmond. Respectfully yours, Saml. Dove, Utica, New York.[1]

Locating their family members proved extremely difficult for the freedpersons. For example, in May 1865, Lucy Bailey, wife of a Michigan soldier in the 100th U.S. Colored Troops, wrote to Secretary of War Edwin M. Stanton concerning the whereabouts of her husband, John, the regiment's drum major. She had not heard from him in three months and, as Lucy informed Stanton, "I am colored it is true but I have feeling as well as white person and why is it the colored soldiers letters cant pass backward and fowards as well as the white ones. . . ." She shared with Stanton her concerns:

I have hurd through others he was very sick and since that I have heard he was dead if he is living I wish you would please grant him afurlogh to come home he was promised one when he went away and he has been gone over ayear and I do wish you would be so kind as to let him come home if he is living I wish you would look oar your Books and see if he is alive I dont know who to write to only you President Lincoln is gone and he was our best friend and now we look to you and I hope God will wach over and protect you through this war[.]

Unfortunately, five days later the War Department informed Mrs. Bailey that almost a year earlier, in June 1864, her husband had "deserted his regiment" and "Nothing further is known in regard to him at this office."[2]

As soon as they were emancipated, former slaves sought to reunite their families, which often had been separated by slave owners for profit or as punishment.

John Q. A. Dennis, a handicapped escaped Maryland slave, also contacted Secretary of War Stanton for help in reuniting his family. Writing from Boston, Dennis explained the tragedy of a family separated by slavery and the difficulties blacks experienced in uniting their loved ones. Dennis informed Stanton:

> I have been in troble for about four yars my Dear wife was taken from me Nov 19th 1859 and left me with three Children and I being a Slave At the time Could Not do Anny thing for the poor little Children for my master ... took me ... some forty mile from them So I Could Not do for them ... the man that they live with half feed them and half Cloth them & beat them like dogs & when I was admited to go to see them it use to brake my heart ... I was keap in Slavy untell last Novr 1863.... So as I have been recently freed I have but letle to live on but I am Striveing ... but what I went too know of you Sir is is it possible for me to go & take my Children from those men that keep them in Savery if it is possible will you pleas give me a permit from your hand then I think they would let them go I Do Not know what better to Do but I am sure that you know what is best for me to Do....
>
> ... will you please excuse my Miserable writing & answer me as soon as you can I want [to] get the little Children out of Slavery, I being Criple would like to know ... if I Cant be permited to rase a Shool Down there & on what turm I Could be admited to Do so No more At present....
>
> John Q A Dennis[3]

The story of twelve-year-old Amy Moore offers yet another painful example that illustrates the difficulties the freedpeople faced in putting their families back together. Amy, her three younger sisters, and her mother were freed by Union troops in Alabama in 1862 and then migrated to Kentucky early in 1863.

Upon entering Kentucky, however, they promptly were reenslaved under a law forbidding freed slaves from coming into that state. Seized by civil authorities and jailed, the Moores then were sold at auction to four different purchasers. Incredibly, the Moores still remained enslaved four months after the end of the war—in August 1865.

Determined to obtain her freedom and that of her sisters and mother, Amy informed officials in Louisville:

> . . . when we arrived at Louisville Ky we were arrested . . . and taken to the Slave pen on Second Street . . . and kept there two or three days when we were taken to the Depot of the Louisville and Nashville RailRoad and there another watchman took charge of us and took us to Shepherdsville Ky and kept us confined several weeks when we were sold at auction by the Sherriff of Bullett County Ky. Dr. McKay bought deponent [Amy] and paid for her the sum of Five Hundred (500) dollars *James Funk* bought deponents [Amy's] mother and youngest Sister paying Six Hundred (600) dollars for the two, and Soon after Sold her mother to *Judge Hoegner* who now holds her as a Slave *James Shepherd* bought my Sister Nora and *Richard Deets* bought my sister Ann. . . .[4]

Amy made her mark—an X—to close the letter.

The U.S. Colored Troops

 Families of slaves who fled their masters to join the U.S. Colored Troops encountered special hardships during both the war and Reconstruction. When the men entered the army they left their wives and children at the mercy of their owners and vulnerable to their reprisals. In 1864, Ann, the wife of a Union soldier from Paris, Missouri, informed her husband of the harsh conditions of life under slavery and cautioned him against sending money in care of her owner, Mr. Hogsett. Ann feared that Hogsett would intercept and keep it.

> You do not know how bad I am treated. They are treating me worse and worse every day. Our child cries for you. Send me some money as soon as you can for me and my child are almost naked. . . . Do not send any of your letters to Hogsett especially those having money in them as Hogsett will keep the money. . . . Do the best you can and do not fret too much for me for it wont be long before I will be free and then all we make will be ours.

Ann signed the letter "Your affectionate wife," and added: "P.S. Sind our little girl a string of beads in your next letter to remember you by."[5]

In May 1866, six black soldiers with families in Kentucky complained of the harsh conditions their families experienced while they served with the U.S. Army along the Texas frontier. According to the leader of the group, G. E. Stanford, "sum of them are Suffren for wanting of healp and Needing of retention. . . . I Know that my own Famuley is Liven in old Kentucky under just as much Slave as the was when I left her or before the war broke out. and agreat mani of other Men's Famuleys is Liven the Same Life." Once freed, the former slaves were "turned out of Doors, and they has no Place to lay thire heads and we has no way to healp them." Summarizing the problems the families of black troops experienced, Stanford informed President Johnson and Secretary of War Stanton:

> Now the old Servant he has no Propty he has no Money he has no House to put them in to. What is they to do now when they is turn out of House and home. I would like to Know how would they go about takeing cire of thire Selfs

and Children. when this Poore old Soldier had nuthing to leave with them. No House to put them in to. the old Servent has Spent the best of his days in Slavery. then must these Poore Creatchers be Sufferd to lye out of Doors Like Beast of sum brute. I says No.[6]

Soon after the end of the war, soldiers of the 36th U.S. Colored Infantry stationed in Virginia wrote General Oliver O. Howard, commissioner of the Freedmen's Bureau, to protest the suffering of their wives, children, and parents who lived in the contraband camp on Roanoke Island, North Carolina. They urged Howard to remove superintendent Horace James and his assistant Holland Streeter. Writing on behalf of their comrades, Richard Etheredge and William Benson explained:

We have served in the US Army faithfully and don our duty to our Country, for which we thank God ... but at the same time our family's are suffering at Roanoke Island N.C.

When we were enlisted in the service we were promised that our wifes and family's should receive rations from goverment. The rations for our wifes and family's have been (and are now cut down) to one half the regular ration. Consequently three or four days out of every ten days, thee have nothing to eat. at the same time our ration's are stolen from the ration house by Mr Streeter ... and sold while our family's are suffering for some thing to eat.

Mr Steeter ... is a througher Cooper head [Copperhead] ... who says that he is no part of a Abolitionist. [He] takes no care of the colored people and has no Simpathy with the colored people. A man who kicks our wives and children out of the ration house or commissary, he takes no notice of their actual suffering and sells the rations and allows it to be sold, and our family's suffer for something to eat.

During and after the war, former slaves who had enlisted in the U.S. Colored Troops protested the treatment of the wives and children they had left behind.

> Captn James ... has been told of these facts and has taken no notice of them ... because it comes from Contrabands or Freedmen the cause of much suffering is that Captn James has not paid the Colored people for their work for near a year and at the same time cuts the ration's off to one half so the people have neither provisions or money to buy it with.
>
> ... our familys have no protection the white soldiers break into our houses act as they please steal our chickens rob our gardens and if any one defends their-Selves against them they are taken to the gard house for it. so our familys have no protection. . . .

The soldiers insisted that they could provide the necessary facts to support their case against James and Streeter. They signed their petition "in behalf of humanity."[7]

Conditions were not much better in Mississippi. Writing in December 1865, Calvin Holly, a black soldier detailed to the Freedmen's Bureau in Vicksburg, reported:

> ... the colored people are in a great many ways being outraged beyound humanity, houses have been tourn down from over the heades of women and Children—and the old Negroes after they have worked there till they are 70 or 80 yers of age drive them off in the cold to frieze and starve to death. . . .
>
> Some are being knocked down for saying they are free, while a great many are being worked just as they ust to be when Slaves, without any compensation. . . . The Rebbles are going a bout in many places through the State and robbing the colered peple of arms money and all they have and in many place killing.

Holly concluded that "the safety of this country depenes upon giving the Colered man all the rights of a white man, and especialy the Rebs. and let him know that their is power enough in the arm of the Govenment to give Justice, to all her loyal citizens—...." Whites, Holly said, were "doing all they can to prevent free labor, and reasstablish a kind of secondary slavery."[8]

Keeping Families Together

Even when their families were reunited, the freedpeople continued to have to fight to keep them together. Under the Black Codes, judges, courts, and U.S. Army officers frequently apprenticed black children—taking them away from their impoverished parents—to work for whites.

These whites assumed wrongly that because blacks were poor they could not provide adequately for their children. Much as they did during the days of slavery, whites believed that they knew what was best for blacks. They concluded—without considering the feelings of the black parents—that the children would be better off under the direction of whites. Commonly this became an excuse for exploiting the labor of the children.

Before the war was over Jane Kamper, a freedwoman from Talbot County, Maryland, learned that her ex-master, William Townsend, was determined to keep her children as apprentices as payment for her own freedom. In order to do so, he locked Kamper's children up so that she could not find them. Before seeking aid from the Army, Jane decided to take matters into her own hands and reclaim her children from Townsend's hold. "I ... got my children by stealth & brought them to Baltimore," she wrote with pride. Forgetting for a moment perhaps that she was no longer a slave, Jane added: "My Master pursued me to the Boat to get possession of my children but I hid them on the boat."[9]

Several months after the end of the war, in another example, Daniel Chase, an ex-slave from Calvert County, Maryland, sought help from the government to regain custody of his five children from Virgil Gant, their former owner. Shortly before Maryland emancipated its slaves in October 1864, the Orphans Court of Calvert County, without permission from Chase and his wife, bound their children to Gant, who thereby hired out two of their sons—seven-year-old Hanson and six-year-old Sias—to other men. Gant received their wages. Despite his appeals, Chase was refused possession of his children.[10]

The case of Tempie Herndon, a slave in Chatham County, North Carolina, ended on a much happier note. Tempie was married to Exter Durham, who lived on a plantation in neighboring Orange County. As slaves the couple had nine children, but Tempie and Exter were allowed to be together only during weekends. Many years after emancipation, Tempie recalled fondly how her family was reunited once the war was over:

> I was glad when de War stopped 'cause den me and Exter could be together all de time 'stead of Saturday and Sunday. After we was free we ... rented de land for a fourth of what we made, den after while we bought a farm. We paid three hundred dollars we done saved. We had a hoss, a steer, a cow, and two pigs, besides some chickens and four geese. Mis' Betsy went up in de attic and give us a bed.... She give us enough goose feathers to make two pillows. Den she give us a table and some chairs. She gives us some dishes too. Marse George give Exter a bushel of seed corn and some seed wheat, den he told him to go down to de barn and get a bag of cotton seed. We got all dis. Den we hitched up de wagon and throwed in de passel of chillen and moved to our new farm, and de chillun was put to work in de field. Dey growed up in de field 'cause dey was put to work time dey could walk good.[11]

Chapter Four

THE FIRST FRIEND: THE FREEDMEN'S BUREAU

"...to make room for complete freedom."

Though Tempie Herndon remembered the emancipation process as a smooth transition to freedom and independence, most blacks described it as a period of intense struggle. Confronted by resentful, vindictive, and often violent white southerners, and in Andrew Johnson an unsympathetic president, the freedpeople desperately needed support, guidance, and protection.

Three months after General Robert E. Lee's men stacked their guns at Appomattox, in August 1865, a black man observed that the freedmen and women in Kansas and Missouri were "all most Thread less & Shoeless without food & no home to go [to] sevral of there Masters Run them off & as fur as I can see the hole Race will fall back if the U.S. Government dont pervid for them Some way or ruther."[1]

During its brief life (1865–1872), the Freedmen's Bureau filled this role, helping to move the South's blacks from slavery to citizenship. Its goal was to assist them in securing and then guaranteeing the blacks' newfound freedom. Throughout Presidential Reconstruction and in the early years of Congressional Reconstruction, the bureau's commissioner, General Oliver O. Howard, worked to ensure that the South's blacks had an equal chance as they began their lives as freedmen and women.

The Role of the Freedmen's Bureau

A federal agency, the Freedmen's Bureau distributed food, clothing, medicine, and medical care to thousands of ex-slaves. It also established schools, hospitals, orphan homes, and churches among them. The bureau provided basic relief to the helpless, the destitute, and the elderly. Never before had a branch of the U.S. government taken on such a social and humanitarian function. Significantly, it assisted the freedmen in arranging labor contracts between themselves and white landowners, who often were their former masters. In addition, the agency arbitrated disputes between the two parties over wages, hours, and conditions of labor. In many cases the Freedmen's Bureau offered the former slaves the first real protection ever allowed them before the law.

General Howard's agency served, according to the Washington *New Era,* a leading black newspaper, as "the first friend of the freedmen, as their champion and defender under military rule, and after the re-establishment of civil authority, as their advocate." Summarizing the bureau's role to the freedpeople, the paper said:

> The Bureau office became in truth a school in which often they learned the first practical business lessons of life. The most satisfactory results at once followed the adoption of the contract system. The freedmen entered into these arrangements with a unanimity and willingness that aston-

ished the most sanguine. Planters generally testify to the industry and good conduct of the freed people. Many demanded that they should be subject to a sort of peonage, or serve an apprenticeship to freedom before being permitted the full autonomy of freedmen ... but all such appeals were wisely resisted.

The *New Era* added that the bureau "rescued" the freedpeople "from hopeless slavery, with its countless perils and since emancipation shielded [them] from great impending dangers."[2]

The *New Era* considered the accomplishments of the Freedmen's Bureau in the field of education as the agency's "crowning work." It was a slow, uphill battle, however, because white southerners violently opposed the idea of educating the freedpeople. According to the paper, "School-houses were burned. In many places the most cultivated and refined teachers were refused board in any white family, or even recognition on the street. They were slandered, vilified, and even in danger of their lives."

Despite such seemingly overwhelming opposition, by 1870 more than 256,000 black students attended more than 4,000 schools taught by more than 9,000 teachers. Each former Confederate state contained at least one college to train black teachers. The *New Era* identified a strong "desire to do something for their own education" among the ex-slaves. "They have contributed lavishly of their poverty to promote the work." In fact, the paper estimated that blacks contributed $200,000 to pay teachers' salaries and build schools.[3]

In Louisiana, black politician Oscar J. Dunn told a congressional committee, the bureau did more than build schools: It protected freedmen and women from being exploited by white planters. He explained:

> The planters ... would make arrangements with them and fail to perform their part of the contract. There have been many instances ... where planters have employed laborers at $15 a month. The contract specified that the planter should be allowed to retain one-half the monthly salary; they would retain it ... until the cotton was picked, and then manage to get into a quarrel with them and drive them away without paying.... I have had several come to me with such information, and some ... I have taken to the Freedmen's Bureau. This is a common thing through all the parishes. The Freedmen's Bureau is a great eyesore to the planters; they do not like it at all.[4]

White farmers and planters objected to the Freedmen's Bureau because the agency took an active role in restructuring postwar southern agriculture. Wartime emancipation was a revolutionary step, one that not only freed the Confederacy's slaves but also began a series of experiments with free labor. During the war northern capitalists employed recently freed slaves on abandoned farms and plantations as wage laborers. The system proved to be profitable for the northerners and introduced black southerners to the idea of free labor.

When the war ended, the South's crops lay in ruins and its economy in shambles. Confederate surrender left several basic economic questions unanswered. Who would control the land? Would the ex-slaves work for their former masters? How would the freedpeople work to support themselves? These economic dilemmas ranked among the most troublesome questions for both blacks and whites during Reconstruction.

Many freedmen, hopeful that the government would compensate them with "forty acres and a mule," refused to work. Some, testing their freedom, looked for new opportunities in the South's towns and cities or in other rural areas. Still others refused to work for those who had only recently kept them in chains. These conditions created a postwar labor shortage.

White southerners, defeated in war, feared for the future of their farms and plantations. They agonized over living among their former slaves and held little confidence that the blacks would make efficient free laborers. Blacks always had been "worked" by whites, who decided which crops to grow and where and when to plant and harvest them. While the blacks had carved out certain areas of "freedom" for themselves even as slaves, they nevertheless remained transportable property, owned and controlled—extensions of their masters' wills. Former fugitive slave and black abolitionist Frederick Douglass summed up the situation under slavery. "The master is always the master," he quipped, "and the slave is always the slave."[5]

Something, then, needed to be done to break the impasse and to begin the reconstruction of the South's agricultural economy. The Freedmen's Bureau seemed to fit the bill in guiding the transition from slavery to freedom for both the former slaves and their ex-masters. Unfortunately, neither side found the government's involvement in economic Reconstruction satisfactory.

The Need for New Reforms

 White farmers and planters complained that the bureau's rule against whites whipping blacks denied them an effective means to discipline their workers. Whites also charged that the government had no right to limit their economic control over the freedpeople. For their part, blacks resented the bureau's regulations that forced them to enter into yearlong contracts with white landholders. They complained that this restricted their freedom of movement and limited their right to take advantage of new economic opportunities.

A Visit from the Old Mistress *by Winslow Homer, 1876.*

Near the end of the war, black freedmen from Louisiana met in New Orleans to present their view of the new conditions brought about by emancipation. Specifically, they protested the labor system established for the Department of the Gulf by General Nathaniel P. Banks and continued by his successor, General Stephen A. Hurlbut. In the official report of their meeting, the blacks charged:

> The labor system established by ... Banks ... does not pratically [*sic*] differ from slavery, except by the interdiction from selling and whipping to death, the laborers.
>
> Some enlargement of the liberties of the laborers was contemplated to gradually take place ... unless Emancipation be a by-word and the boon of freedom a falsehood intended to deceive the world. . . .

Military restrictions, the freedmen added, might have been necessary during slavery, but as the war ground to a close the government's involvement in the economy presented obstacles to the blacks' "complete freedom."

The black Louisianans then passed a series of resolutions summarizing their foremost concerns. It was essential, they said:

> That the right of the employee to freely agree and contract ... with his employer, for the term of labor, is the unquestionable attribute of every freeman.
>
> That as friends of freedom, equal rights, and liberty, we ... protest against every restriction put on ... traveling facilities on account of color.
>
> That we denounce, to the world, the attempts ... of the former slaveowners to transform, the boon of Liberty ... into a disguised bondage.
>
> That while we are prepared for any sacrifice dictated by philanthropy and patriotism, we earnestly protest, against any tax imposed on account of color. . . .

Thus, as Reconstruction got under way, New Orleans blacks made several points abundantly clear. They demanded the right to bargain with employers without outside interference, to work for pay, to travel without restrictions based on skin color, and to be taxed equally and fairly. They refused to be treated like slaves and challenged unfair rules and regulations imposed by the government. Anything less than true equality and opportunity would compromise their freedom.[6]

While these Louisiana freedmen objected to governmental interference with the economy, the vast majority of freedmen and women needed help in coming to terms with their former masters. On the one hand, the former slaves no longer had to work for their ex-masters. They could come and go as they pleased. On the other hand, however, they had to provide for themselves and their children. The blacks no longer could count on laboring for their ex-masters and receiving food, housing, and medical care. And because they were virtually landless and had little money with which to travel or buy land or businesses, blacks across the South were almost forced by circumstance to work for their former captors.

But the blacks nevertheless held some power. White southerners may have controlled the land, but they no longer owned the labor and could not force the blacks to work. Blacks now were their employees, not their slaves. In order to resolve these conflicting interests, the Freedmen's Bureau devised a system whereby the freedpeople and the white landowners signed labor contracts. Though the arrangement was rarely satisfactory to either side, the blacks agreed to work for the whites for one year. In exchange for planting and harvesting the crop, the freedpeople were paid either in cash and a food ration or an agreed-upon share of the crop. The size of "shares" depended on which crop the blacks worked and ranged from as little as one tenth to one fifth of the harvest.

As part of their compensation, white farmers and planters usually allowed the blacks to reside in their former slave cabins. Whites commonly advanced their workers clothing, food, and agricultural tools. They deducted the value of these items from the laborers' share of the crop at harvest time. Two examples illustrate, respectively, planters who paid their freed laborers with cash wages and with "shares."

In 1866 twenty-one freed laborers on Alonzo T. Mial's cotton plantation in Wake County, North Carolina, agreed to

rise at day brake and attend to all duties preparatory to getting to work by Sun rise, and work till Sun Set, and when ever necessary even after Sun Set to Secure the Crop from frost, or taking up fodder or housing Cotton in picking Season after the days work is over, or any other Small jobs liable to loss by not being attended to the night before. Stoping in the . . . Summer months for dinner one hour and a half, at 12 O'C. and in the Fall and Winter [and] Spring months one hour.

That we will do our work faithfully and in good order, and will be respectful in our deportment to . . . [Mr.] Mial and family or [his] Superintendent. . . . That we will attend to all duties necessary to the plantation on Sundays, and will be responsible for the loss or damage from neglect or carelessness of all tools placed in our possession. . . . And we further agree that time lost by idleness or absence without leave shall not be paid for, but for all time So lost we agree to pay double the amount of our wages and that all loss of time from Sickness or absence with leave will not be paid for. Also That we will pay for our rations advanced during all lost time. And we further agree That one half of our monthly wages Shall be retained by The Said Mial till the end of the year, and the amount So retained Shall be forfeited by a violation of this Contract on our part.

... Mial has agreed ... to pay the ... laborers the amount of money pr. month which stands opposite their respective names [on the contract], or in no event payment to be delayed longer than three months, reserving one half however of the above amount till the end of the year.... I also agree to furnish the first day of every month free of charge to every full hand fifteen pounds of Bacon and one Bushel of meal.... I also agree to Sell to them for their family Support ... provisions Such as I may have to Spare at the retail Shop price in the City of Raleigh. I also agree to give them half of every other Saturday between the 1st day of March and the 1st day of August, and will furnish them land for a Small Crop. Also will furnish the teams and tools for the cultivation of the Same provided the teams and tools are not abused by Them.[7]

In 1867 South Carolina rice planter Dr. J. Rhett Motte employed twenty-eight freedpeople, paying them with a "share" of the crop. Careful reading of Dr. Motte's contract with his former slaves shows that he was concerned not only with guarding his share of the profits but also with determining acceptable behavior for the freedpeople who worked for him. Blacks on Motte's plantation agreed

to hire their time & labor on the plantation of the said Dr. J. Rhett Motte from the date of signing this agreement to the first of January, 1868. They agree to conduct themselves honestly & civilly, to perform, diligently & faithfully all such labor on said plantation as may be connected therewith, & which the said Dr. J. Rhett Motte or his agent might require, particularly what is necessary for the raising, harvesting & protecting of the crop. The ... freedmen further agree to bring no ardent spirits ... upon the plantation; also, not to invite visitors upon the premises, or absent themselves ... during working hours, without the consent of the employer or his agent.

The . . . laborers agree to perform reasonable daily tasks on said plantation, & in all cases, when such tasks cannot be assigned, they agree to labor diligently ten hours per day. . . .

For every day's labor lost by absence . . . the laborer shall forfeit fifty cents. If absent more than three days without leave, unless it be on account of sickness or other unavoidable cause . . . [he is] subject to dismissal from the plantation, & forfeiture of his . . . share of the crop. . . .

Said laborers agree to take good care of all utensils, [tools] & implements used on the plantation; also, to be kind [and] gentle to all work animals used for raising the crop; also to pay for any injury done to either the animals or tools while in their hands, & by reason of their own carelessness or neglect.

They agree to keep their houses & garden plots in a neat & orderly manner, & subject to the inspection of the employer or his agent at any time.

In case of sickness among any of the families of the employees, they agree to furnish a nurse from their own number; also a stockminder, if necessary; also, a carpenter, if there be one, to make the necessary plantation repairs in connection with the crop. . . .

The employees agree to furnish from their own number, a foreman, to be selected by the employer or his agent, who shall direct their labors, & shall make report, to the employer or his agent, of all absences, refusal to work, or disorderly conduct, of the employees. The report of the foreman shall be read over, at the end of each week, in the hearing of the people.

The employer agrees to furnish each laborer & his family, with comfortable quarters on the plantation; also, half an acre of ground to each head of a family, and a quarter of an acre to all others, for their own use, & the privilege of getting fire-wood, from some portion of the premises, to be indicated by the employer, or his agent; & each laborer shall be permitted to raise such an amount of poultry & hogs as he can keep upon the premises assigned to him, without injury or annoyance to others.

The employer agrees to furnish a sufficient number of working animals, to feed them at his own expense, & all necessary wagons, carts, ploughs & such other farming implements as cannot be made by the laborers.

Neither party shall sell or use any portion of the crop until after the division of the same, without the consent of the other party.

The crops shall be divided as follows:— To the employees, one-half of the rice produced in the field next to Mulberry, called breakfield; one third of the rice produced from the other fields; also, one third of the corn, peas, potatoes and cotton gathered and prepared for market.

The employer or his agent will keep a book, in which he shall enter all advances made by him to the laborers, & all forfeitures of lost time, which book shall be received as evidence in the same manner as merchants' books are now received in courts of justice. Each employee shall be entitled to a pass book, in which the employer, or his agent, shall make an entry of all advances or rations, & all absences or delinquencies.[8]

Though both the freedpeople and the planters frequently complained about the kinds of labor arrangements outlined by Mial and Motte, on balance, according to Washington's *New Era,* the system of free labor was a dramatic success.

Its present efficiency and success is now such as both to gratify and surprise the friends of the freed people, and to disappoint those who were prophesying evil, and only evil, continually. The common interest of the freedmen with the planter has been demonstrated to both. He has been furnished good and increasingly reliable laborers. Since the inauguration of the new system of labor the South has raised about two million bales of cotton per year. . . . *The last cotton crop is represented by the press as the most valuable ever grown.*[9]

Freedmen's Bureau agents, overworked and underpaid, played a major role in supervising the South's new system of agriculture. While many of these men, including blacks from the North, were committed to protecting the freedpeople and to treating both blacks and whites fairly, some clearly sided with the landowners. According to the New Orleans *Tribune,* the organ of Louisiana's Republican party, Freedmen's Bureau agents in that state discriminated against black laborers. The editor complained that "under the present state of things, there is hardly any justice for a poor man. The laborer on the plantations is, to a very great extent, in the clutches of his employer. Should he be abused or wronged what are the means of redress? Practically he has none."

If he goes to the Bureau's agent, he finds there an officer who rides with his employer, who dines with him, and who drinks champaign [*sic*] with him. He is not likely to receive impartial justice at the hands of such a prejudiced officer. Most of the Agents think their particular business is to furnish the planters with cheap hands, and as a consequence to retain at any cost the laborers on the plantations. They are, in fact, the planter's guards, and not nothing else. . . .

It is, therefore, perfectly useless for the poor laborer to look at the Freedmen's Bureau for relief. He knows in advance that the Bureau will send him back to his unjust or exacting employer. He will not be assisted to get his pay, or to get redress; but will be told to go back to his master and do his work.

As a solution, the editor urged that the government appoint attorneys to protect poor blacks in each of Louisiana's parishes.[10]

Despite this and other criticisms, blacks generally regarded agents of the Freedmen's Bureau as their friends. Dr. Daniel Norton, a New York-trained black physician who practiced in Virginia during Reconstruction, feared the recrimination that the freedpeople would face if the Freedmen's Bureau and the U.S. Army left the South. Responding to the questions of a congressional committee, Dr. Norton replied that, should representatives of the government leave the South, "I do not think that the colored people would be safe. They would be in danger of being hunted and killed. The spirit of the whites against the blacks is much worse than it was before the war."[11]

Chapter Five

A SECOND BONDAGE: THE PLANTATION SYSTEM

"...wee want a Friend."

Even when the new system of labor agreements worked fairly for both sides, contract labor rarely enabled the freedpeople to get what they really wanted: small farms of their own. No matter how hard they worked, during Reconstruction most blacks remained landless, poor, undereducated, and subject to white control. Over time freedpeople became trapped in perpetual debt by what became known as the sharecropping and farm tenantry systems.

Under both systems of labor whites held title to the land. Sharecroppers were equipped with supplies and worked small family-size farms. On average, they shared one-half of the crop with the landlord. Farm tenants provided their own supplies and shared a smaller percentage of the crop (approximately one third) with the white landowner.

Under both systems the freedpeople bought food, clothing, and supplies on credit from white-owned plantation stores. Blacks frequently were overcharged for what they purchased and underpaid for the crops they produced. Accumulating ongoing debt to the owners of the land they worked, generations of blacks became tied to the land. They could not leave until they had paid off their debts. If the blacks failed to do so, they were liable to arrest and imprisonment. Whites thus controlled not only the land but also gradually regained control of the South's black work force.

A South Carolina black politician, the Reverend Francis L. Cardozo, explained in 1868, that following emancipation the plantation system replaced slavery in keeping blacks in a painful grip. "We will never have true freedom until we abolish the system of agriculture which existed in the Southern States," he explained. "It is useless to have any schools while we maintain this stronghold of slavery as the agricultural system of the country." Postwar conditions reminded him painfully of slavery. Blacks and their white friends had to hammer out constitutional protection for the freedpeople. Cardozo reminded members of South Carolina's constitutional convention that

> as colored men, we have been cheated out of our rights for two centuries, and now that we have the opportunity, I want to fix them in the Constitution in such a way that no lawyer ... can possibly misinterpret the meaning. If we do not do so, we deserve to be, and will be, cheated again. Nearly all the white inhabitants of the State are ready at any moment to deprive us of these rights, and not a loophole should be left that would permit them to do it constitutionally.[1]

After two centuries of servitude whereby they and their ancestors had worked on the land of whites, the freedpeople were determined to own their own land. General Sherman's 1865 "Special Field Orders, No. 15" promised to allot "not more than forty acres of tillable ground" for each freed family and set aside abandoned and confiscated land—islands and coastal lands from Charleston, South Carolina, to the St. Johns River in Florida—for that purpose. The government's hope was that if the blacks would occupy the land for three years, then they could purchase it and establish self-governing communities.

By mid-1865, about 40,000 freedpeople occupied 300,000 acres of land in the area designated by Sherman. Whites, however, the original owners of the land, soon challenged the freedpeople's right to the tracts. Supported by President Andrew Johnson, in March 1866, white planters were allowed to return and occupy their land. Federal troops forcibly removed those blacks who believed that they had "a right to the land." Meanwhile the government instructed the freedpeople to sign labor contracts with their former masters.

By late 1866, only 1,565 of the 40,000 freedpeople who had occupied land retained possession of their tracts. Unable to secure their own land, most blacks worked for white planters under labor contracts. But some blacks protested.

Claims for Land Ownership

The freedmen and women on South Carolina's Sea Islands, for example, were furious. These people believed that they had been tricked and that their chances of obtaining land were slipping away. As early as 1864 residents of St. Helena Island had petitioned President Lincoln, accusing plantation superintendent Edward S. Philbrick of deceiving them and complaining about abusive treatment by one of his agents. Philbrick had promised to sell land to the blacks but later refused to do so. The freedmen and women wanted to know why the Lincoln administration agreed to sell such a large amount of land to men like Philbrick in the first place, when longtime residents like themselves were eager to buy it. In their petition, they informed the President:

> Wee the undersigned. beleaveing wee are unfarely delt with, Are led to lay before you . . . our greaveiences. . . . wee . . . beeg, though it may be long, You will beare kindly with [us]; Reade & answere uss, And as now so, henceforth, our prayrs shall asscende to the Throan of God, for your future suceess on Earth. & Tryumph in Heaven.
>
> For what wee have receaved from God, through you, wee will attempt to thank you. . . . Wither our freedom is for ever or a day, wither as Slaves or Freemen, wee shall ever, carry you & your kindness to us in our hearts. . . .

The petitioners then listed their grievances against Philbrick who, the freedpeople charged, "bought up All our former Masters Lands under falls pretences." Before purchasing the land Philbrick had assured the ex-slaves that he would resell it to them at the price of $1 per acre. Once taking control of the land, however, Philbrick refused to sell it. He intended to offer the plots at $10 per acre—a price that few of the former slaves could afford.

Clearly frustrated with Philbrick, the blacks emphasized how he maintained seemingly total control over them.

> He will not sell us our Land neither pay us to work for him; And if wee wish to work for others where wee might make something, he turns us out of our Houses, he says wee shall not live-on his plantation unless wee work for him. . . .
>
> Why did Goverment sell all our Masters Land's to Mr Philbrick for so trifling a sume; we are all redy . . . to buey all our Masters Land, & every thing upon them; and pay far more than he did for them. . . .

Outraged that they could not get title to their own land, the ex-slaves enclosed a petition signed by nineteen freedmen listing their grievances against Philbrick. They insisted that "Wee have work'd for Mr Philbrick the whole year faithfully, and hav received nothing comparatively, not enough to sustaine life if wee depended entirely uppon our wages." In addition to controlling the land and the workers' wages, Philbrick also owned the stores that sold supplies to the workers. They complained that in them he charged "feerefull prices for every nessary of life." Landless and unable to obtain the goods they wanted, "the People have become discouraged, all most heart broken."

In addition to economic control, the freedpeople reported a case of severe treatment by Charles Ware, one of Philbrick's managers, that they said "exceedes anything done in our Masters time." According to their petition, in order to punish a woman for some infraction, Ware "turn'd the cloths of a Colard Girl over her head turned her over a Barrel, & whipd her with a Leathern Strap." The blacks considered the case so "shamefull" that "wee blush [to] write or send it [to] you." Nonetheless, they insisted, "the truth must be told."

The South Carolina blacks demanded that Philbrick be forced to honor his promises and sell them as much land as they wanted at a fair price. If he refused, then the freedpeople wanted the government to purchase the land from Philbrick. They would then supply their own seed and tools, farm the land, and pay the government one half of the crops they raised as rent. Such an arrangement, the blacks said, would be preferable to working for Philbrick. They guaranteed the government that once freed of Philbrick's control, they would be most productive—"there will be but few feet of Ground Idle. As Mr Philbrick has broken his part of the contract," the blacks asked, "is [the] Government bound to keep thers?" Finally, the petitioners requested that the government send a fair and just agent to the freedpeople, one "who will see not wrong; but right done us one who will deal justly by us, Wee doo not want a Master or owner Neither a driver with his Whip wee want a Friend."[2]

Throughout Reconstruction, land reform became a hotly contested political issue for South Carolina's blacks. In 1865 the Reverend Richard H. Cain, who later served two terms in the U.S. House of Representatives, demanded that the federal government distribute the confiscated plantations to the freedpeople. "Let them have homesteads. . . . Then we shall see the Southern States blooming. The cotton fields and rice plantations will produce as never before, . . . and universal prosperity will reign supreme."[3]

In South Carolina's 1868 constitutional convention Cain argued persuasively for governmental assistance so that the freedmen could acquire land. Cain described the condition of the ex-slaves as "most deplorable." Slavery left them poor and homeless, he said, a condition worsened later by crop failures and the nonpayment of blacks by white employers. Most could not afford to buy tools and seed. Such circumstances thus made them "wards" of the federal government. Because of this, Cain believed, the U.S. government should appropriate one million dollars to buy land for South Carolina's ex-slaves. Cain proposed

> that said lands . . . shall be sold to the freedmen as homes, in parcels of 10, 20, 40, 50, 60, 80 and 100 acres, to suit the purchasers; . . . and that when said lands are so purchased and sold, the purchaser thereof shall enter into an obligation to the Government to pay the amount of the value of the said land purchased . . . from the Government, and the Government should hold claim to said lands . . . and at the expiration of five years the person so purchasing shall make full payment.

During the debates over South Carolina's new state constitution, Cain repeatedly emphasized the importance of land ownership by blacks. In his opinion, home ownership held the key to the advancement of the race.

> I believe the possession of lands and homesteads is one of the best means by which a people is made industrious, honest and advantageous. . . . it is a fact well known, that over three hundred thousand men, women and children are homeless, landless. The abolition of slavery has thrown these people upon their own resources. . . . As long as people are working on shares and contracts, and at the end of the year are in debt, so long will they and the country suffer. But give them a chance to buy lands, and they become steady, industrious men.

Land, according to Cain, would empower the ex-slaves. Blacks objected to working for whites because they distrusted them. Again and again their former masters cheated them out of the fruits of their labor. Once the freedpeople owned their own farms, however, Cain predicted that they would labor, thereby disproving "one of the arguments used against us, that the African race will not work." Cain was unconvinced that "the black man hates work any more than the white man does. Give him a place to work, and I will guarantee before one year passes, there will be no necessity for the Freedmen's Bureau."[4]

"Nothing in Slavery as Mean as This"

 By 1872, landless South Carolina blacks grew impatient. They blamed white Republican leaders for failing to provide them with "forty acres and a mule." "Kush" (a pseudonym based on a biblical reference to blacks) and other members of the state's Young

Men's Progressive Association, a black organization, complained that after seven years of Reconstruction, few South Carolina blacks owned their own land. He explained:

> Four hundred thousand people who were slaves before the war do not even now own their labor. Their labor is owned by the land owner who controls and directs it.
>
> And so long as the labor of the working rural people is controlled by their employer, just so long must the people be in a state of squalid, wretched poverty.
>
> So soon as each family possess a small homestead farm, just so soon does it become independent and the controller of its own labor, and able to fix and to a great extent, regulate the price for labor.

"Kush" complained that white Republicans, determined to hold office, had deceived the freedpeople into believing that they would acquire land. They were nothing more than "negro-hating imposters and demagogues" who needed to be ousted from office. "There was nothing in slavery as mean as this," "Kush" insisted, "because slavery was honest in its intentions and purposes, and meant what it said and did; but this is open contempt, and he who, among us, submits to it, should be despised by the whole colored race, as unworthy of its confidence." "Kush" not only charged white Republicans with misleading the blacks, but he also accused them of stealing state and federal funds targeted for their uplift.

To remedy these problems, "Kush" urged blacks to replace their corrupt leaders with honest whites and blacks. Once in office the new leaders would authorize the state of South Carolina to purchase 80,000 homesteads of 10 acres each for the freedmen and women. The blacks would have four years to pay back the state.

Land ownership would be a boon for South Carolina's blacks, "Kush" insisted. It would transform South Carolina into a virtual oasis. He explained:

> So soon as the little farm is secured, each family can commence to improve by ditching, manuring, planting fine little orchards of half an acre or more, or various choice fruits, such as peaches, pears, plums, apples, and even currants and gooseberries as garden fruits; all ... if well selected ... will ... thrive. ...
>
> So soon as the farm is paid for, the farther improvement of the neat handsome homestead cottage with sufficient conveniences, neatly paled and fenced ... which must take the place of the old plantation quarters, or "nigger houses" as the people used to call them, ... all must most materially enhance the valuation and price of the lands in all parts of the state.[5]

Despite such appeals, by the end of Reconstruction in 1877 it was clear that the U.S. government would make no effort to distribute public lands among the freedpeople. In most cases former owners regained title to their property. Incredibly few of the emancipated slaves received their own land. Historian Claude F. Oubre writes that though some freedpeople did acquire homesteads, "those who secured land during the first years of freedom were the exception rather than the rule, probably less than 5 percent of the total Negro population." Far and away most remained landless.[6]

An Exodus

 Discouraged and doubtful that they would ever acquire their own land and become independent farmers in the South, some freedpersons decided to abandon their native region to settle on homesteads on public land in the West. Late in 1872, Washington's *New National Era* encouraged black Georgians to seek refuge out West. By moving away, blacks would rid themselves of the sharecropping system and its unending cycle of poverty. There they could purchase cheap farmland and escape the terrorism of white nightriders such the Ku Klux Klan. According to the editor,

> Emigration can only result in a benefit to the colored people. In the Territories they will be free, and the time now in part attempting to elude the vengeance of the Ku-Klux Klans of chivalrous Georgians, can be wholly devoted to the bettering of their condition, without fear of molestation. The land settled upon by the emigrant will be his own, the profits accruing from energetic labor will fill his coffers, his children can be educated in peace, and he loses nothing of his American citizenship by the removal to the plains.[7]

As appealing as this might sound, during Reconstruction such appeals fell largely on deaf ears. Not until the famous "Exodus" of March 1879, did approximately 15,000 blacks emigrate to Kansas. They came principally from four states—Mississippi, Louisiana, Texas, and Tennessee. Fortunately in 1879–1880 the black migrants, poorly clothed and poorly equipped for farm work, encountered an unusually mild winter on the Kansas plains. A black preacher who journeyed to Kansas remarked that "God seed dat de darkeys had thin clothes an' He done kep' de cole off." Historian Nell Irvin Painter explains that though the "Exodusters," as they were called, "remained relatively poor," in general they "were far freer and less discriminated against than were their peers in the South."[8]

On To Liberty *by Theodor Kaufmann, 1867.*

The vast majority of the freedpeople, however, refused to leave the South. It was the land of their slave ancestors and the only land they knew. And the great distances and transportation costs involved made mass migration totally impractical. Though the inability of blacks to obtain their own land remained a long-festering sore, in the next century many landless blacks left the rural South for economic opportunities in northern cities. In the meantime, black southerners looked for local political solutions to their immediate economic and social problems.

Chapter Six

ORGANIZING FOR EQUAL RIGHTS

"These are no ordinary circumstances."

Though their circumstances generally were improved from slavery times, the freedpeople during Reconstruction still had relatively few options. Migrating from the South was impractical. Except for the Freedmen's Bureau, the U.S. government offered them little help. And they constantly were surrounded by hostile whites who resented their new free status. Faced with these harsh realities, the South's former slaves concluded that they would have to organize politically in order to enjoy the fruits of their new freedom. They would have to help themselves.

The active participation of black southerners in post-Civil War politics was a remarkable and exciting, if not revolutionary, result of emancipation and Reconstruction. In November 1865, for example, South Carolina blacks met at Zion Presbyterian Church in Charleston to set forth their political agenda. Those who attended the blacks' Colored People's Convention were determined to be treated justly. Though former free blacks dominated the convention, ex-slaves also attended. Both demanded equal treatment before the law, equitable taxation, the vote, and the right to bear arms. While they assured whites that they would obey the law, the blacks complained:

> Without any rational cause or provocation on our part . . . we . . . have been virtually . . . excluded from . . . the rights of citizenship, which you cheerfully accord to strangers, but deny to us who have been born and reared in your midst, who were faithful while your greatest trials were upon you, and have done nothing since to merit your disapprobation.
>
> We are denied the right of giving testimony in like manner with that of our fellow-citizens, in the courts of the State, by which our persons and property are subject to every species of violence, insult and fraud without redress.
>
> We are also . . . not only denied the right of citizenship, the inestimable right of voting for those who rule over us in the land of our birth, but by the so-called Black Code we are deprived . . . the right to engage in any legitimate business free from any restraints. . . .
>
> You have by your Legislative actions placed barriers in the ways of our educational and mechanical improvement; you have given us little or no encouragement to pursue agricultural pursuits, by refusing to sell us lands, but . . . bring foreigners to your country and thrust us out or reduce us to a serfdom, intolerable to men born amid the progress of American genius and national development.
>
> Your public journals charge the freedmen with destroying the products of the country since they have been made free, when they know that the destruction of the products was brought about by the ravages of war. . . . How unjust, then, to charge upon the innocent and helpless, evils in which they had no hand. . . .

The black South Carolinians looked backward to the Declaration of Independence as a precedent for their demands for equal treatment. Though this document stated that "all men are created equal," the former slaves complained that their people always had been denied equal rights. They listed just some of the "wrongs" that whites had committed against them.

> We have been deprived of the free exercise of political rights, of natural, civil, and political liberty.
>
> The avenues of wealth and education have been closed to us.
>
> The strong wall of prejudice, on the part of the dominant race, has obstructed our pursuit of happiness.
>
> We have been subjected to cruel proscription, and our bodies have been outraged with impunity.
>
> We have been, and still are, deprived of the free choice of those who should govern us, and subjected unjustly to taxation without representation, and have bled and sweat for the elevation of those who have degraded us, and still continue to oppress us.

The freedpeople who attended the Colored People's Convention were serious and determined to obtain equal rights. They realized that not until they were accorded the same constitutional rights as whites would they attain real freedom.[1]

The Constitutional Conventions

 In March 1867, less than two years after the blacks received their freedom, the U.S. Congress passed the first Reconstruction Act. This bill authorized ten of the former Confederate states to draft new constitutions based on black suffrage as well as the Fourteenth Amendment. These would frame basic laws and include universal manhood suffrage. Delegates to the state constitutional conventions were to be elected by males "of whatever race, color or previous condition." This unprecedented move (in 1868 only eight northern states permitted blacks to vote and none had large black populations) guaranteed that freedmen would have the right to vote in all of the ex-Confederate states. Acceptance of the new state constitutions by the U.S. Congress would be among the prerequisites for readmission to the Union.

Blacks considered the constitutional conventions essential to the attainment of equal rights in their states. On May 3, 1867, soon after the U.S. Congress authorized that blacks should be registered to vote, a convention of former slaves and free Negroes met in Mobile, Alabama, and passed the following resolutions:

> Whereas, lately the right of suffrage has been bestowed on our race, heretofore held in bondage, in order that we may acquire political knowledge that will insure us protection in our newly acquired rights,
>
> Whereas, it seems to be the policy of our political oppressors to use unfair and foul means to prevent our organization and consolidation as a part of the Republican Party in Alabama,
>
> *Resolved,* that we proclaim ourselves a part of the Republican Party of the United States and of the State of Alabama. . . .[2]

On August 1, 1867, instead of going to work, thousands of blacks in Richmond, Virginia, went to the First African Baptist Church to attend the Republican state convention to draft a platform for the upcoming state constitutional convention. As a result, many local tobacco factories, lacking the bulk of their work force, shut down for the day. As the December 1867 constitutional convention approached, the freedpeople—housekeepers, farmers, mechanics, and laborers—participated in parades, rallies, mass meetings, and the convention itself. They were determined to be involved in planning for their future.

In Arkansas, for example, where only eight freedmen were elected to the state's 1868 constitutional convention, the blacks nonetheless participated actively in debate. They responded openly and directly to whites who insulted their race. James T. White, a Baptist minister, demanded equal suffrage, schools for blacks, and prohibitions against racial discrimination on public conveyances. He considered "the ballot . . . our only means of protection." Though the new state constitution failed to contain everything he desired, White nevertheless supported the finished document. "I vote Aye," White said, because

> My race having waited with patience, and endured the afflictions of slavery of the most inhuman kind, for 250 years, today I find a majority of a Constitutional Convention, that is willing to confer upon me what God intended that I should have. I contend, friends, that the elective franchise is a God-given right, which comes to every man born into the world—be he black or white, green or gray, little or big, it is his right. . . .
>
> Another reason why I shall vote . . . for the Constitution, is, that I see in it a principle that is intended to elevate our families—the principle of schools—of education. That is the only way that these Southern people can be elevated. Were they properly educated they would not to be led, from prejudice, to oppress other men. Were they educated, they would not hate us because we have been slaves.[3]

Louisiana's large black and mulatto population watched the proceedings of its state constitutional convention closely. The freedmen, who constituted a majority in the convention, wanted assurances that they would get the vote, that former rebels would be disfranchised, and that public facilities would be integrated. According to the New Orleans *Tribune,*

> The conventionists are well conscious of the responsibility they will incur; they are well aware of the vast consequence of the task laid before them. These are no ordinary circumstances. The whole country—nay, the whole world, are watching our moves, to decide whether popular government, in its most complete sense, is practicable or not. The people who elected the delegates have . . . recently been freed from bondage. They were not raised as freemen, but as slaves, without the benefits of education and almost outside of the pale of society. They know little; they are unexperienced; they are illiterate. The right of suffrage was not conferred upon them on account of their superior education or peculiar fitness but simply as a high homage to the rights of man. . . . How have these newly enfranchised citizens exercised the right of suffrage? They have shown . . . that they were able to distinguish patriots from demagogues, and men of liberal principles from sycophants and traitors.

The goal of the new constitution would be to achieve "variety in unity," blending those of different ethnic origin, race, class, education, language, religion, and physical strength.[4]

Soon after, Louisianans of both races began the difficult task of writing their new state constitution. The editor of the New Orleans *Tribune* reminded delegates that their foremost responsibility was to secure political and civil rights for the state's freedpeople. Anything less would be an insult to those who gave up their lives in the revolutionary struggle for emancipation. He explained:

> The main object to be realized by the Constitution about to be made is evidently to secure the full enjoyment of their rights to the formerly disfranchised and oppressed citizens. This is the paramount duty which devolves upon the Convention now in session. It is, in fact, to attain that aim that the revolution has been made. What would have been that revolution without the abolition of slavery and the enfranchisement of the black and colored men? The blessings of freedom, the enjoyment of civil and political liberties, existed previous to the war, as far as the caucasian race was concerned.
>
> Take back the extension of the right of franchise and the abolition of slavery, and we shall return to the state of things which existed prior to the rebellion. All other rights are subsidary to these first elementary rights and depending upon them.[5]

Once Louisiana's new constitution was drafted, the state held elections and ratified the Fourteenth Amendment. It was readmitted to the Union in June 1868.

Freedmen also had a majority in South Carolina's constitutional convention, and they spearheaded a model new constitution in the Palmetto State. The delegates overhauled the state's laws and crafted a truly democratic foundation for the future. The document enfranchised the former slaves, protected their economic rights, and established a free public school system. During its proceedings, black delegate Jonathan J. Wright, a lawyer, Republican party organizer, and later state supreme court justice, declared "that the object of the Convention is to give every man an equal chance before the law, and then if he does not show himself a man, then the fault is his and cannot be charged to the Convention." Wright added: "It is our duty to destroy all the elements of the institution of slavery. If we do not, we recognize

The South Carolina legislature, 1873.

the right of property in man." He realized the importance of the moment—the chance "to lay a foundation that will be for the general welfare of the people in all future time." Wright noted: "We are not framing a Constitution for to-day, but for years, and we should be careful how we execute that task."[6]

The Reverend Richard H. Cain agreed. When debating the question of voting rights, he explained:

> I would not deprive any being, rich or poor, of the enjoyment of that franchise, by which alone he can protect himself as a citizen. Whether learned or ignorant, he is subject to government, and he has an inalienable right to say who shall govern him. . . . He may not understand a great deal of the knowledge that is derived from books; he may not be generally familiar with the ways of the world; but he can, nevertheless, judge betwen [sic] right and wrong, and to this extent he has as much ability to cast his vote and declare his opinion as any other man, no matter what may be his situation in life. It has too long been the right of tyrants to rule over man and prescribe for him a line of action, and never again will this right be conceded to any class, especially in South Carolina, where, as I believe, we have entered upon a new era, . . . In remodelling the institutions of the country, we propose to establish them on a broad basis, so that the halo of liberty may overshadow every class of men, and no right however small, shall be withheld from those entitled to enjoy it. . . . One of the greatest reasons why I feel thankful to my Maker for the present condition of things, is that it has opened to us an age of progress, in which mankind will take a forward bound towards humanity, developing its purest principles and bringing out its greatest results.

Cain believed that the new constitution promised a better life for future generations of black South Carolinians.[7]

Others agreed. During South Carolina's constitutional convention, Alonzo J. Ransier, a black journalist from Charleston, argued in favor of compulsory education for children in his state. According to Ransier,

> If there is any one thing to which we may attribute the sufferings endured by this people, it is the gross ignorance of the masses. . . . Had there been such a provision as this in the Constitution of South Carolina heretofore, there is no doubt that many of the evils which at present exist would have been avoided, and the people would have been advanced to a higher stage of civilization and morals, and we would not have been called upon to mourn the loss of the flower of the youth of our country.[8]

Another delegate, Jonathan J. Wright, pointed to the seemingly universal demand for education among the freedpeople. He reported:

> The great cry throughout the State has been, send us teachers, send us men, send us women, who will teach us how to read and write, and we will pay them for it. The people are hungry and thirsty after knowledge. They seem inspired with spirit from on high that tells them knowledge is the only source by which they can rise from the low and degraded state in which they have been kept.[9]

Though blacks and white Republicans were removed from positions of power in South Carolina in the late 1870s, the constitution that Wright, Cain, Ransier, and others drafted remained in place until 1895, decades after they were dislodged from office. It testified to their dedicated labors.

Chapter Seven

THE RIGHT TO VOTE

"It is their day of jubilee."

Once the new southern state constitutions were in place, the freedmen prepared to participate in politics. Before they could do so, however, they had to become enfranchised—to receive the right to vote. Before the Civil War only five northern states permitted black men to vote. Thousands of northern blacks still were denied suffrage as late as 1869. But southern black leaders and their northern friends considered the vote essential for the freedpeople if they were ever to rid the South of the spirit of slavery. From the moment of their emancipation the freedmen waged an aggressive campaign to assure that they would vote. South Carolina's Jonathan J. Wright, for example, urged his fellow black leaders to "instill into the mind and hearts" of the freedmen "the sacredness of the ballot-box. The people must be taught that the votes they hold in their hands are their only great defense of the rights and privileges which God has granted to man."[1] Indeed, black southerners considered the vote to be among the sweetest fruits of emancipation.

Just weeks after Confederate General Robert E. Lee surrendered at Appomattox, a group of freedmen from Newbern, North Carolina—former soldiers, ex-slaves, and freeborn blacks—wrote President Andrew Johnson, informing him of their determination to vote.

> Some of us are soldiers and have had the privilege of fighting for our country in this war. Since we have become Freemen, and have been permitted the honor of being soldiers, we . . . feel that we are men, and are anxious to show our countrymen that we can . . . fit ourselves for the creditable discharge of the duties of citizenship. We want the privilege of voting. It seems to us that men who are willing on the field of danger to carry the muskets [in time of war] . . . in the days of Peace ought to be permitted to carry the ballots . . . we cannot understand the justice of denying the elective franchise to men who have been fighting for the country, while it is freely given to men who have just returned from four years fighting against it.[2]

Freedmen in Montgomery, Alabama, informed General Howard of the Freedmen's Bureau that their lives were controlled by poverty, suffering, and harsh treatment by their former masters. When Howard asked the blacks what remedy they proposed, most said that the only true solution to their problems was the vote. One elderly ex-slave came forward and explained:

> Every creature has got an instinct—the calf goes to the cow . . . the bee to the hive. We's a poor, humble, degraded people, but we know our friends. We'd walk fifteen miles in war time to find out about the battle; we can walk fifteen miles and more to find out how to vote.[3]

The influential New Orleans *Tribune,* the voice of blacks in the lower Mississippi Valley, defined the franchise as a sign of the blacks' manhood. According to the editor,

> Neither labor nor fighting has proved to be too much for our race. We labored long and hard. What riches the soil of the Southern States has yielded for two hundred years, has grown up through the exertions of our arms and the sweat of our brows. What triumphs the Union armies have gained in the field, to secure the integrity and perpetuity of the Republic, was obtained through our efficient and powerful help. . . . We now ask why we should not be treated as men.[4]

The *Tribune* reminded blacks that as freedmen they no longer had to rely upon white politicians for support and protection. Armed with the vote, blacks could establish schools for their children and create political offices for their leaders. Times had indeed changed, the editor explained.

> We now have to ballot, to use it on our own behalf. We have more than the ballot; we compose a majority in the State, and with the help of our Radical friends, we compose a majority in the Convention. We are, therefore, able to make the law; we have not to receive it from anybody. It is for us to promise situations to our friends—to the trusty ones; it is for us to distribute offices and favors. We will put into office those in whom we have confidence; . . . the colored masses are the masters of the field.[5]

The South's freedmen became enfranchised thanks to the first Reconstruction Act of March 2, 1867. Whereas some white southerners were disenfranchised for disloyalty, black southerners were permitted to vote in elections for the various state constitutional conventions. Throughout the South, agents of the Freedmen's Bureau registered black voters, and the freedmen prepared to vote for the first time. Genuine democracy seemed to lie on the horizon.

Led by black teachers and ministers from the North, they held mass meetings, barbecues, and parades to learn about politics and to celebrate this special moment. The ex-slaves had a seemingly insatiable appetite for voting. By the end of 1867, 700,000 blacks, in contrast to 660,000 whites, were registered to vote. Black voters played an important role in electing Ulysses S. Grant president in the election of 1868.

While applauding this, the New Orleans *Tribune* cautioned its readers not to seek vengeance against whites. It questioned the wisdom of denying former Confederates the right to vote. To be sure, the courts should deny the vote to men convicted of war crimes. But the editor considered disenfranchisement a dangerous precedent, one that might someday be used against the blacks. Instead of depriving whites of the vote, then, blacks should stand committed to "equal liberties and equal rights."

> We want the suffrage and the eligibility—no distinctions in office nor in officers. We want to elect colored justices and colored members of the General Assembly in parishes where meritorious candidates from the African race, can get a majority. But we want to fight that political contest squarely and fairly, . . . and not by . . . suppressing the minority.
>
> We shall not jeopardize our claims to political rights by denying those rights to any class of citizens as a class. Every man, in a community, has interests to protect. Oppression grows from the permanent disfranchisement of a class of the people. We have suffered oppression, and we do not ask to throw off the yoke to put it on the shoulders of others. Our republic must be grand and pure, and while majorities shall rule, minorities must have a voice.[6]

Most blacks, however, were more concerned with their own right to vote than with the problems of former Confederates. For example, because Kentucky had remained loyal to the Union during the Civil War, blacks in the state were exempted from the provisions of the Reconstruction Acts. Kentucky blacks thus were denied the suffrage provisions awarded freedmen in the former Confederate states. Outraged by their exclusion, 170 former black soldiers petitioned the U.S. Congress in July 1867.

> The undersigned, citizens (colored) of the United States of America, respectfully present this our petition, to humbly ask your Honorable Assembly to grant us the right of Suffrage.
>
> Your petitioners . . . are residents of the State of Kentucky, by whose laws they are denied the right to testify in Court, &c. And . . . many crimes have been committed upon them during the last year, for which they have failed to obtain redress. Colored men have been frequently murdered in cold blood by white citizens, and as we have not the right to testify against them, the criminals go unpunished.

The former black troops then declared their "*unquestioned* Loyalty" to the U.S. government, which, they argued, had subjected "them to the malevolence of the friends of the 'Lost Cause.' " Former Confederates charged that blacks were "too ignorant to prudently exercise the great boon of freedom." But whites, too, lacked education, according to the black veterans, and they were entitled to vote. The petitioners argued "that men vote their political convictions, not their intellectual acquirements. We are poor, but not paupers." To support this point the blacks listed the amount of property taxes they paid in the state. In sum, the blacks said, enfranchising them would "arrest the cruel spirit of robbery, arson and murder in Kentucky, as it most evidently has done in more Southern States."[7]

The Power of the Vote

The Kentuckians referred to the upsurge of violence during Congressional Reconstruction as whites tried to curb black advancement. In response, black Republicans reminded their constituents to take heed—to use their hard-fought ballots to elect their friends and to defeat their enemies. According to the editor of Washington's *New National Era,* a black-owned newspaper,

> Colored voters of the South you must not forget those who forget you and your rights. You must teach them that they are mistaken in considering you mere voting machines, ready and willing to vote for any man calling himself a Republican, ... Southern Senators are urging amnesty for rebels ... preferring this to justice and protection to loyalty, they certainly do not represent the ever loyal colored element in the South, and when opportunity offers the colored people should see to it that neither Senator nor Representative shall further misrepresent them in Congress. Do not vote for a member of Congress who does not aid in giving you "Equality before the law."[8]

Black voters followed this advice and elected numerous blacks to public office throughout the South. In the period 1867–1877, roughly 2,000 freedmen held federal, state, and local public offices. Seven former Confederate states sent blacks to the U.S. Congress—two to the U.S. Senate and fourteen to the House of Representatives. All through the region blacks won high-ranking state posts—one governor; six lieutenant governors; 112 state senators; 683 state representatives. Others served on the state and county level as cabinet officers, superintendents of education, militia officers, justices of the peace, city councilmen, sheriffs, judges, and numerous other posts. Most were elected by constitu-

HARPER'S WEEKLY.

A JOURNAL OF CIVILIZATION.

VOL. XI.—No. 568.]   NEW YORK, SATURDAY, NOVEMBER 16, 1867.   [SINGLE COPIES TEN CENTS.
[$4.00 PER YEAR IN ADVANCE.

Entered according to Act of Congress, in the Year 1867, by Harper & Brothers, in the Clerk's Office of the District Court for the Southern District of New York.

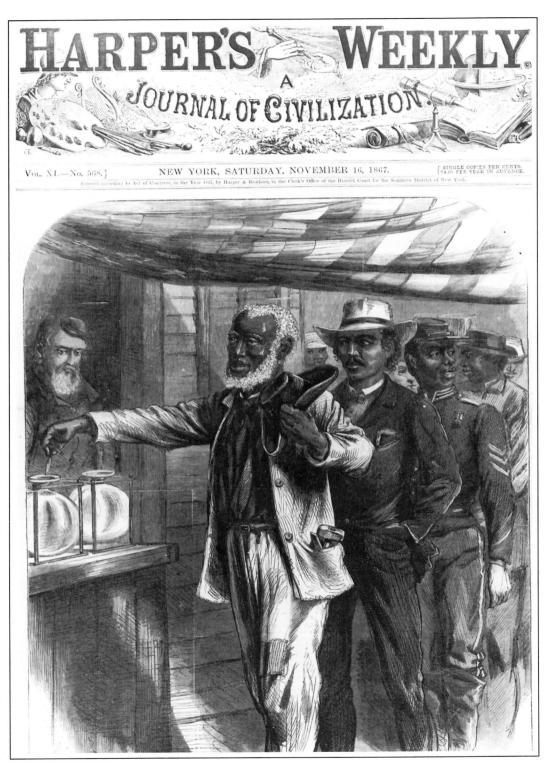

This wood engraving by A. R. Waud depicts freedmen triumphantly casting their first ballots after receiving the right to vote in 1867.

encies where blacks composed majorities. South Carolina, Mississippi, and Louisiana—states with the largest black populations—elected the largest number of black officeholders. All through the South, men who only a few years previous had been slaves were elected to federal and state offices.

Armed with the vote (the Fifteenth Amendment was adopted by Congress in 1869 and ratified by the states in 1870), during Congressional Reconstruction thousands of black southerners participated in politics in every former Confederate state. In addition to serving in elected and appointed positions, they organized Union Leagues, Grant Clubs, and other grass-roots political organizations. These helped to educate blacks about politics, promoted Republican party candidates, and accompanied black voters to the polls on election day.

Mifflin Gibbs, a black judge from Little Rock, Arkansas, described a typical Republican campaign tour in rural areas of the South during Reconstruction.

> The speakers, with teams and literature and other ammunition of political warfare ... would start at early morn from their respective headquarters on a tour of one or two hundred miles, filling ten or twenty appointments. Good judgment was necessary in the personal and peculiar fitness of the advocate. For he that could by historic illustration and gems of logic carry conviction in a cultured city would be "wasting his sweetness on the desert air" in the rural surroundings of the cabins of the lowly. I have heard a point most crudely stated, followed by an apposite illustrative anecdote, by a plantation orator silence the more profuse cultured and eloquent opponent. ... The meetings, often in the woods adjoining [a] church or schoolhouse, were generally at a late hour, the men having to care for their stock, get supper, and come often several miles; hence it was not unusual for proceedings to be at their height at midnight.[9]

Obstacles and Accusations

 Though often highly competent and successful in the political arena, black officeholders nonetheless frequently faced discrimination from hostile whites. In 1868, for example, the white majority in Georgia's legislature expelled its thirty-two elected black members. White politicians argued that although freedmen had received the right to vote, the new state constitution did not expressly give them the right to hold office.

Outraged by the expulsion of their elected officials, blacks met in Savannah, Georgia, to protest and to seek intervention by the U.S. government. According to the freedpeople, the expulsion was

> an unjust deprivation of our most sacred rights as citizens, a high-handed outrage on a large political element in this community, in direct contravention of the voice of a majority of the legal voters of the state as expressed at the ballot-box, and contrary to the plain letter and spirit of the reconstruction acts, under which the constitution of Georgia was framed, adopted, and presented for congressional acceptance.

They argued that justice would never be served "while such fraudulent and unrepublican proceedings of the legislature are permitted to remain valid and of binding force." They underscored "the persecutions we have suffered, the barbarities committed in the name of the law . . . by those in power by virtue of the action of said legislature." In their opinion, conditions under "freedom" were but "only another and worse form of slavery."[10]

Obviously determined to remove blacks from office by any means—fairly or unfairly, peacefully or violently—white Democrats commonly charged that during Reconstruction black Republicans were corrupt and held too many political positions. Both allegations were incorrect, a Louisiana black editor argued. In the first months of Radical Reconstruction, he explained,

> we find the offices in the hands of white men, almost exclusively. Out of two hundred mayors in this State, there is ONE who belongs to the African race. In the whole State of Louisiana, there can be found in office thirty-five or forty colored men. The balance is white. And moreover God knows under what pressure, under what hopes of getting colored votes for the white officers who made the appointments, these few colored men were put into office. It should be remembered also that after election day, the appointing heads having lost their election, many a colored officer was turned out of his situation.[11]

Modern scholars agree that during Reconstruction black politicians represented their constituents honestly and performed their work creditably. According to historian Eric Foner, "Nowhere in the South did blacks control the workings of state government, and nowhere did they hold office in numbers commensurate with their proportion of the total population, not to mention the Republican electorate. Nonetheless, the fact that ... blacks occupied positions of political authority in the South represented a stunning departure in American government."[12]

Ironically, one of the more insightful assessments of black politicians during Reconstruction came from a harsh white critic—journalist James S. Pike. Though opposed to slavery since the 1840s and, later, a Republican political appointee, Pike nevertheless disliked blacks as individuals and strongly opposed universal black suffrage. Upon visiting South Carolina in 1873, he ridiculed black politicians in the state legislature—their language, their appearance, and their behavior.

Unlike other white racists, however, Pike understood the importance of politics to the freedpeople. Able to look beyond his own racial biases, Pike realized that the blacks' outward appearances hid

> something very real. . . . It is not all sham, nor all burlesque. They have a genuine interest and a genuine earnestness in the business of the assembly which we are bound to recognize and respect, unless we would be accounted shallow critics. They have an earnest purpose, born of a conviction that their position and condition are not fully assured, which lends a sort of dignity to their proceedings. . . . Seven years ago these men were raising corn and cotton under the whip of the overseer. To-day they are raising points of order and questions of privilege. They find they can raise one as well as the other. They prefer the latter. It is easier, and better paid. Then, it is the evidence of an accomplished result. It means escape and defense from old oppressors. It means liberty. It means the destruction of prison-walls only too real to them. It is the sunshine of their lives. It is their day of jubilee.[13]

Chapter Eight

THE FIRST LEADERS

"I am here to demand my rights. . . ."

Who were the almost 2,000 blacks who held political office during Reconstruction? What were their offices? What were their concerns? Where did they live and work? Why did they enter politics?

The blacks who tried their hands at reconstructing the South were a talented and diverse lot. Just over one half had been slaves. But many of those who had been enslaved were freed by their masters, by self-purchase, or by running away prior to the war. Almost one half of the black officeholders were free men before the war. Twenty-two of them had owned slaves themselves. Many of the black officeholders were light-skinned mulattoes. More than a hundred were black "carpetbaggers," men who came from the North in search of political opportunities. Collectively, the men plied a broad range of trades—farmers, professionals, artisans, laborers, and small businessmen.

South Carolina had the largest number of black officeholders during Reconstruction. Blacks composed seventy-one of the delegates to the state's 1868 constitutional convention. South Carolinians elected 6 persons of African descent to the U.S. House of

Representatives, 29 to the state senate, and 210 to the state house of representatives. There were two black lieutenant governors, one state treasurer, two secretaries of state, one supreme court justice, two state land commissioners, and two speakers of the house. Other states had equally impressive numbers of black politicians. As a group the men were aggressive, determined, and committed to elevating their race.

George Teamoh, Virginia

George Teamoh (1818–1883), for example, was an ex-slave shipyard carpenter from Virginia who served in his state's constitutional convention, 1867–68, and state Senate, 1869–1871. A mulatto devoted to uplifting all blacks, Teamoh sought to reform his state's penal system, especially the tradition of whipping blacks as a punishment for crime.

In order to remove the vestiges of slavery, he said, and "in the name of republican civilization," Virginia had to replace its outdated laws. Teamoh explained:

> Sir, one may be sent to the penitentiary for a number of years, and from thence return to peaceful society with his person unscarred; but the whipping post and cowhide, mingling man's heart's blood with the outer covering of the beast, dooms him, or her, black or white, poor, but not the rich, to a life of shame, written in red colors on the back.
>
> Why, sir, we whip one for stealing a chicken, and then turn him loose on society like Samson's foxes, with firebrands, ten-fold more the child of devilish incendiarism than ever he was before, if formerly so inclined. He dives deep into his hell of revenge, and from cool calculation will have it, if it costs him his head.

> And judging from the past, *whipping settles nothing,* but only harrows up and brings out what was really in the man—the evil of his heart—the evil of his heart.

Teamoh not only considered whipping a barbaric and uncivilized pratice, but he knew that during Reconstruction it was used exclusively to punish blacks, not whites. In a democracy, he said, punishments must be fair, just, and humane and be applied equally to all classes and races.[1]

Robert Brown Elliott, South Carolina

Robert Brown Elliott (1842–1884), a dark-skinned free black from England, came to South Carolina in 1867, passed the bar, and served in the state's constitutional convention. In that body he fought vigorously for universal manhood suffrage and to provide compulsory education in South Carolina's new constitution. In Elliott's view, states had the responsibility to educate their people without discrimination. He believed passionately that equal education for all children lay at the heart of a democracy. Though whites objected to their children going to school with blacks, Elliott brushed off that issue as irrelevant. He argued that education would help South Carolinians of all races.

After listening to a debate on the merits of state-funded schools, he remarked:

> The only question is whether children shall become educated and enlightened, or remain in ignorance. The question is not white or black united or divided, but whether children shall be sent to school or kept at home. If they are compelled to be educated, there will be no danger of the Union, or a second secession of South Carolina from the Union. The masses will be intelligent, and will become

Robert Brown Elliott.

the great strength and bulwark of republicanism. If they remain uneducated, they will inevitably remain ignorant, and ... ignorance is the parent of vice and crime, and was the sustainer of the late gigantic slaveholder's rebellion. . . .

It is not a question of color, but simply ... whether white or black shall keep their children at home uneducated, bringing them up in ignorance, useless to society, or be compelled to send them to school, where they can be made intelligent and useful in the community where they reside.[2]

An effective political organizer and campaigner, Elliott served two terms in the South Carolina House of Representatives (1868–1870, 1874–1876) and the U.S. House of Representatives (1871–1874). In 1874, Elliott recalled the thrill of delivering his first speech in the U.S. Congress.

> I shall never forget that day, when rising in my place to address the House I found myself the centre of attraction. Everything was still. Those who believe in the natural inferiority of the colored race appeared to feel that the hour had arrived in which they should exult in triumph over the failure of the man of the "despised race" whose voice was about to be lifted in that chamber. The countenances of those who sympathized with our cause seemed to indicate their anxiety for my success, and their heartfelt desire that I might prove equal to the emergency. I cannot, fellow-citizens, picture to you the emotions that then filled my mind.[3]

As pioneers in breaking down racial barriers, Elliott and other Reconstruction-era black officeholders encountered much discrimination from whites. In 1871, for example, a white U.S. Treasury Department employee objected when seated in a Washington, D.C., restaurant next to Elliott. Unwilling to accept the slight, he promptly had the man fired from his government post.

Pinckney B. S. Pinchback, Louisiana

 Pinckney B. S. Pinchback (1837–1921) was one of the most able but controversial black officeholders of the Reconstruction era. Certainly, his political career ranks among the most complicated.

Son of a Mississippi planter and a free black woman, the light-skinned Pinchback spent his youth as a steward on a Mississippi riverboat. He received a commission as an officer during the Civil War to recruit U.S. Colored Troops but resigned twice because of discriminatory treatment by whites. Pinchback urged blacks to demand suffrage if "they wanted to be men." Settling in Louisiana after the war, he was elected to the state's 1868 constitutional convention, where he supported free schools, universal suffrage, and equal treatment for persons of all races on public transportation and by businesses. After serving in the state Senate (1868–1871), Pinchback became lieutenant governor in December 1871, when the incumbent died. Following Governor Henry Clay Wormoth's impeachment, Pinchback served a brief term (December 9, 1872–January 13, 1873) as acting governor. He was the first black in U.S. history to hold this office, and not until 1990 would the nation have another black governor.

Following his stint as governor, Pinchback was elected both to the U.S. House of Representatives and the U.S. Senate. His opponents, however, contested both elections. After long delays, Pinchback ultimately lost both claims to office. During his entire career he was plagued by charges of political corruption. Convinced that he was treated unfairly, Pinchback defended his right to be seated in Congress. He believed that he had been deceived by white Republicans who opposed qualified blacks—men "with intelligence, cultivation, and sagacity"—in favor of less qualified whites. Pinchback explained:

> The colored people have begun to understand this trick and to appreciate intelligence among their class, and to realize that they are held responsible for bad governments in the South; and I say if you will let them alone and only treat them with fair play ... they will work out their own salvation. When they understand that all bad laws, all peculations, iniquities, frauds, and corruption which are

Pinckney B. S. Pinchback.

charged upon these governments will at last be laid upon their shoulders and they will be held responsible for the same, in my judgment they will be swift to move in the right direction to rectify any wrongs which may exist by the selection of honest, intelligent and competent men to administer the affairs of the Government.[4]

James D. Lynch, Mississippi

James D. Lynch (1839–1872), born in Baltimore, Maryland, was the son of a free mulatto merchant and a slave mother purchased by his father. A minister of the African Methodist Episcopal Church, Lynch preached to black troops during the Civil War and organized black congregations during Reconstruction. In 1865 he blamed the bloody Civil War on slavery, which brought down God's wrath upon the country.

> All that my race asks of the white man is justice.... The white man may refuse us justice. God forbid! But it cannot be withheld long; for there will be an army marshalled in the Heavens for our protection, and events will transpire by which the hand of Divine Providence will wring from you in wrath, that which should have been given in love.[5]

Settling in Mississippi, Lynch worked tirelessly as a missionary, establishing schools and churches for his race, and for the Freedmen's Bureau. A member of the secret Union League, he organized black Republicans in the state and urged them to vote and engage in politics. In 1869 Lynch was elected secretary of state, one of five blacks in Mississippi to hold that post during Reconstruction. He worked aggressively and spoke eloquently in favor of integrated public schools. A white writer who opposed Lynch's politics was nevertheless fascinated by the black man's oratorical "style."

> He was a remarkable man.... He was a great orator; fluent and graceful, he stirred his great audiences as no other man did or could do. He was the idol of the negroes, who would come from every point of the compass and for miles, on foot, to hear him speak. He rarely spoke to less than a thousand, and often two to five thousand. He

swayed them with as much ease as a man would sway a peacock feather with his right hand. They yelled and howled, and laughed, and cried, as he willed. I have heard him paint the horrors of slavery ... in pathetic tones of sympathy till the tears would roll down his cheeks, and every negro in the audience would be weeping; then wiping briskly away his tears, he would break forth into ... the blessings of emancipation, and every negro in the audience would break forth in the wildest shouts. There was a striking peculiarity about this shouting. Imagine one or two thousand negroes standing *en masse* in a semi-circle facing the speaker; not a sound to be heard except the sonorous voice of the speaker ... and [all] of a sudden, every throat would be wide open, and a spontaneous shout in perfect unison would arise, and swell, and subside as the voice of one man; then for a moment a deadly silence would follow, and every eye would be fixed on the speaker as he resumed, until all of a sudden the mighty shout would rise again, and again. . . .[6]

Henry McNeal Turner, Georgia

Henry McNeal Turner (1834–1915), a mulatto, was born a free black in South Carolina. Ordained by the African Methodist Episcopal Church, he served during the Civil War as chaplain in the U.S. Colored Troops. Years later he was elected one of the church's twelve bishops. Turner came to Georgia in 1865 as an agent of the Freedmen's Bureau but spent most of the Reconstruction years as a minister and politician. In 1867 he was elected to Georgia's constitutional convention and a year later to the state legislature. Like other black delegates, Turner was expelled from Georgia's House of Representatives in 1868. Responding to his removal, Turner declared: "I shall neither fawn nor cringe before any party, not stoop to *beg* for my rights.... I am here to demand my rights, and to hurl thunderbolts at the men who dare to cross the threshold of my manhood."[7] In 1870, Congress ultimately reseated Turner, along with Georgia's other black legislators.

In 1871, Turner summarized his work in a speech before the African Methodist Episcopal Church's Georgia Annual Conference.

> I first organized the Republican party in this State, and have worked for its maintenance and perpetuity as no other man in the State has. I have put more men in the field, made more speeches, organized more Union Leagues, Political Associations, Clubs, and have written more campaign documents that received larger circulation than any other man in the state.... And ... these labors have not been performed amid sunshine and prosperity. I have been the constant target of Democratic abuse and venom, and white Republican jealousy. The newspapers have teemed with all kinds of slander, accusing me of every crime ... I have even been arrested and tried on some of the wildest charges, and most groundless accusations ever distilled from the laboratory of hell. Witnesses have been paid as high as four thousand dollars to swear me in the penitentiary; white preachers have sworn that I tried to get up insurrection,... a crime punishable with death, and all such deviltry has been resorted to for the purpose of breaking me down—and with it all they have not hurt a hair of my head,... I neither replied to their slanders nor sought revenge ... I invariably let them say their say, and do their do; while they were studying against me I was studying for the interest of the Church, and working for the success of my party,... So that up to this time my trials have been a succession of triumphs. I have enemies, as is natural, but at this time their tongues are silent, and their missles are chaff, while my friends can be counted by hundreds of thousands.[8]

In addition to his legislative position, Turner also served terms as postmaster and customs inspector, respectively, at Macon and Savannah, Georgia. After years of fighting racism, racial violence, and discrimination, late in the century Turner concluded that black Americans would have better lives in Africa than in America. Abandoning hope for racial justice in this country, he urged blacks to emigrate to Africa.

Robert C. DeLarge, South Carolina

Robert C. DeLarge (1842–1874), a mulatto, descended from a South Carolina free black tailor who owned slaves and a woman of Haitian ancestry. During Reconstruction he worked for the Freedmen's Bureau in South Carolina and was a leading voice in the state's 1868 constitutional convention. Committed to promoting racial harmony, DeLarge emphasized the mutual interests of blacks and whites. In 1868 DeLarge urged men of both races to support South Carolina's new constitution. He explained:

> Whatever tends to injure the white man also injures the colored race, and I appeal to the whites to cooperate with us. The new constitution asks for the sacrifice of no principle. The true men of my race proved by the Constitution that they desired to oppress no one. I ask ... that you whites come forward and bridge over the breach, which should not exist. If the whites would prove that they are willing to extend to others the rights which they desire for themselves, they would be met in the same spirit. If they will come forward ... they will find us ready to meet them.[9]

Elected to South Carolina's House of Representatives in 1868, DeLarge held several important posts—chairman of the ways and means committee and head of the state land commission. In 1870 he ran for the U.S. Congress, promising, if elected, to "demand for my race an equal share everywhere."[10] He won and served in the House of Representatives until 1873.

Benjamin F. Randolph, South Carolina

Benjamin F. Randolph (1837–1868), a free mulatto from Kentucky, attended Ohio's Oberlin College and served as a chaplain in the U.S. Colored Troops during the Civil War. Applying for a

Benjamin F. Randolph.

position with the Freedmen's Bureau in 1865, he explained: "I don't ask position or money. But I ask a place where I can be most useful to my race."[11]

South Carolina fit the bill. In the Palmetto State, Randolph served as assistant superintendent of schools for the Freedmen's Bureau, organized black Republicans for the Union League, and worked as a journalist. He rose quickly in Republican party circles. In 1868, as a delegate to the state's constitutional convention, Randolph drafted laws that guaranteed all citizens, irrespective of race and color, equal political rights. He favored a bill of rights that finally would destroy all distinction based on race and previous condition of servitude. Randolph argued that South Carolina's black majority—"ground down by three hundred years of degradation—must have their political rights protected." He added that "all of my radicalism consists in believing one thing, namely, that all men are created of one blood; that 'God created all nations to dwell upon the earth.'"[12] After the convention Randolph chaired South Carolina's Republican party. In October 1868, while campaigning in Abbeville County, Randolph was assassinated by members of the notorious terrorist group the Ku Klux Klan.

Chapter Nine

RACIAL TERRORISM

"I will stick to the republican party and die in it."

The Ku Klux Klan began in 1865 in Pulaski, Tennessee, as a social group. Six ex-Confederate soldiers in search of fun organized it. They devised the name "Ku Klux" (after the Greek word for circle, *kuklos*) and added "Klan" because the originators supposedly came from Scotland and Ireland. During Reconstruction new groups of Klansmen, called "dens," emerged, first in Tennessee and then throughout the South. A Grand Cyclops headed the dens. A Grand Wizard commanded the order. The secret group had several levels of officers: Night Hawks, Goblins, Furies, Hydras, and Geni. Ordinary members were called Ghouls. They masked their identity with hoods and white robes.

During Congressional Reconstruction the Klan changed from a social group to a terrorist political organization. At first Klansmen hoped to frighten the freedmen and their white Republican supporters, to discourage them from voting and holding office. When this tactic failed, however, they used violence. According to historian Allen W. Trelease, after 1867 the Klan became "a counter-revolutionary device. . . . For more than four years it whipped, shot, hanged, robbed, raped, and otherwise outraged Negroes and Republicans across the South in the name of preserving white civilization."[1]

Whites deeply disliked the participation of blacks in politics, often venting their frustration in violent ways. Whites expressed their anger at the loss of their slaves directly at the freedpeople. Whites not only resented the loss of their property, but they also missed the racial and social control that they had held over their slaves. Throughout Reconstruction, Klansmen and other white terrorists resorted to racial violence. They used lynching—whipping, torturing, then murdering—to control blacks and to return the Democrats to power.

During Reconstruction former slaveholders confronted workers—their ex-slaves—who challenged their authority by demanding equal treatment and pay. When other forms of intimidation—verbal abuse and driving them away without food or pay—failed to intimidate the blacks, whites resorted to violence to discipline their former slaves. Lewis H. Douglass, son of Frederick Douglass and editor of the Washington *New National Era,* likened the brutality of postwar racial violence to the old system of slavery. "The barbarism of slavery," he wrote in 1874, "is constantly being exemplified by the atrocities perpetrated in obedience to the lingering spirit of that accursed institution."[2] Numerous cases from throughout the South prove Douglass's point.

Riots and Random Violence

 In 1866, bloody race riots erupted in Memphis, Tennessee, and New Orleans, Louisiana, in May and July, respectively. A government committee investigated the Memphis riot, which lasted three days, and described it as

Scene in Memphis, Tennessee, during the riot on the morning of May 2, 1866, sketched by A. R. Waud.

an organized and bloody massacre of the colored people of Memphis, regardless of age, sex, or condition, inspired by the teachings of the press, and led on by sworn officers of the law composing the city government, and others. The mob, . . . under the protection and guidance of official authority, . . . proceeded with deliberation to the commission of crimes and the perpetration of horrors which can scarcely find a parallel in the history of civilized or barbarous nations, and must inspire the most profound emotions of horror among all civilized people.[3]

During the disturbance forty-six blacks died, eighty-five were wounded, and at least five black women were raped. Whites either stole or destroyed over $130,000 worth of black-owned property. Lucy Tibbs, the pregnant wife of a black riverboat man, was one of the victims. Testifying before the Joint Committee of Fifteen on Reconstruction, she described the wanton shooting of blacks by whites, the burning of their schools and homes, and the anguish of being physically assaulted. From her home she observed five blacks murdered. "Just where I live," Lucy told the committee, "when the greatest fight was going on . . . there were, I should think, four hundred persons in the crowd. They were just firing at every colored man and boy they could see."[4]

In New Orleans, thirty-four blacks were killed in the riot, and hundreds more were wounded. General Philip Sheridan, who commanded the Department of the Gulf, remarked that the New Orleans riot "was an absolute massacre by the police . . . a murder which the mayor and police of the city perpetrated without the shadow of a necessity." Even worse, Sheridan said, the riot "was premeditated."[5]

Race relations were so tense that the city was ready to explode like a tinderbox. Following the riot Oscar J. Dunn, an ex-slave who later was elected Louisiana's lieutenant governor, informed a congressional committee that New Orleans blacks still feared that they had no protection from the city government. Whites insulted them publicly and brushed up against the freedmen on the streets trying to provoke fights.

The freedpeople experienced similar violence in smaller communities throughout the South. In 1866 the Reverend William Thornton, a literate former slave from Hampton, Virginia, told a congressional committee of widespread violence in Elizabeth City County, Virginia. In one instance a white man shot a freedman who had accidentally cut down a tree on his land. The white man was imprisoned but then quickly was released. In another instance a black husband and wife were whipped by whites because they had gone to hear Thornton preach. Former Confederates in the area considered the minister a threat to their social order because he advised the former slaves to marry and act like free men and women. Whites also threatened to destroy Thornton's church and to murder him.

Similar conditions existed in the state of Maryland where former Confederate soldiers made life unbearable for the freedpeople. In March 1866, Charles A. Watkins, a former soldier, wrote to General Howard of the Freedmen's Bureau because, he said, "we donot know who elce to look to but you." Watkins explained that

> the returned colard Solgers are in Many cases beten, and their guns taken from them, we darcent walk out of an evening if we do, and we are Met by Some of these roudies. that were in the rebbel army they beat us badly and Sumtime Shoot us.

Watkins cited an example. On March 7, 1866, he said,

> our collard School teacher was collard and beaten, he got loos and ran and was Shot at. the party was Six white Men. and on Sunday evening the 11th Sum persons we think

> two in Number cam on horse back to out chirch a bout 11 oclock P M and Set fier to te chirch that we keep School in and burnt it to the ground.

In conclusion, Watkins expressed his desperation:

> Now—Sir—this is the way we get our freedom can you do any thing for us. for gods Sake do it we do not know where to go for Safty.[6]

The Ku Klux Klan

As Congressional Reconstruction unfolded, members of the Ku Klux Klan committed numerous acts of racial violence. In 1868, for example, Arkansas Klansmen murdered more than 300 Republicans, including U.S. Congressman James M. Hinds. Before Louisiana's 1868 election, Klansmen killed no fewer than one thousand people. The Klan was so popular in New Orleans that roughly one half of the city's adult white male population belonged to the organization.

In South Carolina, ex-slave Lorenzo Ezell of Spartanburg County recalled that "by '68 us was havin' such a awful time with de Klu Klux." At first they tried to scare the freedmen by pretending to be the ghosts of dead Confederate soldiers.

> Dey all dress up in sheets and make up like spirit. Dey groan around and say dey been kilt wrongly and come back for justice. One man, he look just like ordinary man, but he spring up about eighteen feet high all of a sudden. Another say he so thirsty he ain't have no water since he been kilt at Manassas Junction. He ask for water and he just kept pourin' it in. Us think he sure must be a spirit to drink dat much water. Course he not drinkin' it, he pourin' it in a bag under he sheet.

Though Ezell's family moved to another location, they could not escape the Klan.

Dey claim dey gwine kill everybody what am Republican. My daddy charge with bein' a leader amongst de niggers. He made speech and instruct de niggers how to vote for Grant's first election. De Klu Klux want to whip him and he have to sleep in a hollow log every night.

De Klu Klux come to us house one night, but my daddy done hid. Den I hear dem say dey gwine go kill old man Bart. I jump out de window and shortcut through dem wood and warn him. He get out de house in time and I save he life. De funny thing, I knowed all dem Klu Klux Spite dey sheets and things, I knowed de voices and dey saddle horses.

Dey all knowed I knowed dem den, but I never told on dem. When dey seed I ain't gwine to tell, dey never try whip my daddy or kill Uncle Bart no more.[7]

In May 1869, Emanual Fortune, a former slave and member of both Florida's 1868 constitutional convention and its legislature, testified before a U.S. congressional committee investigating the Klan. Fortune said that Klan outrages and the inability of the state government to prevent violence forced him to leave his home in Jackson County, Florida. Blacks and white Republicans were frequent targets of Klan shootings. When asked why he left, Fortune explained:

There got to be such a state of lawlessness and outrage that I expected that my life was in danger at all times, and I left on that account; in fact I got, indirectly, information very often that I would be missing some day and no one would know where I was, on account of my being a leading man in politics, and taking a very active part in it.

Fortune then told that Klansmen objected to the idea of blacks voting. They believed that "the damned republican party has put niggers to rule us and we will not suffer it." These whites were willing to take the law into their own hands rather than live under what they considered to be Republican and black misrule. In their opinion, the only legitimate government would be a "white man's government."[8]

In August 1869, Klansmen visited the Alabama home of ex-slave tailor George S. Houston determined to kill him. A representative from Sumter County in the state legislature, Houston registered black voters, helped organize the Union League, and encouraged blacks to stand up to whites. After the whites wounded his son and broke down the door to Houston's home, one Klansman entered and shot him in the thigh. Grabbing his gun, Houston

> cocked the barrel, and shot at his head at fifteen steps, but it was only squirrel shot. My wife jumped and fastened the window. Then they shot the window full of holes and the side of the house beside that. As she shut the window the balls came in the house like rain. They shot the whole side of the house, and balls fell inside of the house all along. I was lying patient. The next day the people came in and picked the balls where they had fallen inside of the house through the plank.

Rescued by armed blacks, Houston fled the county and lost all of his property. His attackers went unpunished. Despite his problems, Houston remained committed to the Republican party and believed that the future of the freedpeople lay in its hands. "I am a republican, and I will die one," he said.

> I say the Republican party freed me, and I will die on top of it. I don't care who is pleased. I vote every time. I was

register of my county, and my master sent in and lent me his pistols to carry around my waist when I was register, to protect myself against my enemies. I am a republican to-day, and if the republican party can't do me any good, I will never turn against it. I can work in the cotton-patch and work at my trade, and get along without any benefit from my party, and so I will stick to the republican party and die in it.[9]

Throughout 1869, Klansmen in North Carolina, where Republicans had won convincing electoral victories, whipped and beat black officeholders. In 1870 they played a major role in overturning Republican party control in Georgia. In 1871 Klansmen in Mississippi went on a rampage, burning black schools and churches, and torturing and killing teachers.

In May of that year, for example, the Klan terrorized fifty-two-year-old Elias Hill, a crippled ex-slave from York County, South Carolina. A preacher, teacher, and president of the local chapter of the Union League, Hill was a prime target for Klan violence. One night six Klansmen broke into his cabin. The disguised men believed that Hill, who could not walk and had the use of only one arm, had burned houses and farm buildings belonging to whites. When he denied their charges, the Klansmen beat Hill repeatedly, dragged him across the yard, and searched his home for incriminating documents. None surfaced.

Frustrated by their lack of success, the Klansmen threatened to murder Hill but then decided to whip him until he was almost unconscious. "I was so chilled with cold lying out of doors so long and in such pain I could not speak to pray," he said. The white terrorists next attacked Hill's black neighbors—whipping men and women, raping one woman, and burning one of their cabins. Blacks in the community were so alarmed that most refused to stay in their homes at night. The Klansmen had accomplished their goal of intimidation.[10]

In 1871, Robert Gleed, a former slave and later a Mississippi state senator, testified before a congressional subcommittee, condemning the activities of white terrorists and explaining why such criminals rarely were brought to trial. He described racial violence in Mississippi as a "reign of terror." The Klan's purpose, in his opinion, was

> to remand the colored men of the country to as near a position of servitude as possible, and to destroy the republican party if possible.... We believe it had two objects, one was political, and the other was to hold the black man in subjugation to the white man, and to have white supremacy in the South;... and then we have evidence of it from the parties who have sworn and bound themselves together under oaths, ... in clubs, to do all they can from year to year, and from month to month, as long as they live, to establish white supremacy in Mississippi, and the disenfranchisement of the black man.

According to Gleed, not only were Mississippi blacks denied basic civil rights, but whites viewed those who protested as "insolent." In other words, whites considered it an offense for blacks to stand up for their newfound constitutional rights.[11]

Justice

Unfortunately, senseless outrages and lawlessness—whippings, rapes, and torture of blacks—appeared all too commonly during Congressional Reconstruction. In September 1874, "Watchman," a black correspondent who used this pseudonym to protect his identity, reported on the rash of atrocities committed against freedpeople in Augusta, Georgia. Whites mobbed an innocent black man; a white policeman knocked a pregnant black woman to the ground for no apparent offense; white vigilantes dragged a black prisoner from his prison cell, shot him, and then riddled his dead body with bullets; a white man stabbed a black man to death for no apparent crime; and Ku Klux Klansmen unsuccessfully tried to assassinate an officer in Augusta's black military company. In each case the white perpetrators either evaded punishment altogether or received an insignificant penalty. Whites in Augusta not only exhibited little respect for blacks, but understood that the two races would receive unequal treatment before the law. Blacks, in other words, were persecuted, while whites went unpunished.[12]

Similar conditions existed elsewhere in Georgia. Writing from the northern part of the state, Custas Morum, a freedman, explained that Ku Klux Klansmen warned blacks that if they voted in the 1874 election they would be killed. Morum, a teacher in a country school, explained that black Georgians desperately sought civil-rights legislation. Day in and day out, he said, blacks who committed no crimes were denied "the right of trial by our own people, subjected to severe punishment in the penitentiary and in many instances death at the hands of ignorant white jurors."[13]

"U," an unidentified black correspondent from Nashville, Tennessee, identified comparable conditions in his state. Whereas whites, he complained, blamed blacks for conducting a "war of races," in fact no such thing existed. According to "U,"

There is no war of races going on in the South, and not likely to be. In these disturbances the negro is never the aggressor, but acts on the defensive. What is going on at present is a massacre of negroes by Southern white men who fancy themselves wronged by the Senate passing the civil rights bill, and they seek to be revenged upon us. Our only crime is that we are negroes. We are outraged by these cowards because we are in the minority and are loyal to that Government which subdued the rebels and triumphantly established the nation's flag upon the ruins of the Southern Confederacy.

He next described what constituted "a real carnival of crime" during August 1874 directed at Tennessee blacks. Whites burned black churches and schools and whipped and tortured black men and women, many in broad daylight. Their "only crime," explained "U," "is that they are negroes." Just one white man had been arrested. Because white Tennesseans would go to any lengths to maintain supremacy, he believed that only the U.S. Army could protect the freedpeople.[14] Across the South the freedpeople looked to the federal government for help.

Chapter Ten

THE PROMISE OF EDUCATION AND A HOMELAND

"We are not free."

Before the Civil War the federal government played a minimal role in the lives of Americans, north and south. Because of the upheavals of the war, however, during Reconstruction the government entered the lives of black southerners as never before. The three Reconstruction amendments to the U.S. Constitution—the Thirteenth, Fourteenth, and Fifteenth—were major steps forward in achieving equal rights for the freedpeople. Although powerful on paper, however, the amendments lacked means of enforcement to guarantee that the former slaves would remain truly free and enjoy the full measure of citizenship.

On the local level the Freedmen's Bureau and the U.S. Army guarded the ex-slaves' hard-earned freedoms. To help them further, the federal government in 1870 and 1871 passed three Enforcement Acts designed to strengthen the Fourteenth and Fifteenth Amendments. This legislation protected the right of blacks to vote and outlawed terrorist groups like the Ku Klux Klan. The federal government also assisted in educating and integrating the freedpeople into southern society.

During Presidential Reconstruction the freedmen and women had a blind faith that education, like "forty acres and a mule," suddenly would empower and elevate their race. In April 1865, the New Orleans *Black Republican* announced: "Freedom and school books and newspapers, go hand in hand. Let us secure the freedom we have received by the intelligence that can maintain it."[1] Education for the freedpeople began years before, as early as 1861, when northern philanthropic organizations and churches sent missionaries to areas of the South occupied by Union troops. Former slaves considered education the key that would unlock years of ignorance and liberate their minds as well as their bodies.

School Doors Open

 After the war the Freedmen's Bureau and northern freedmen's aid societies opened schools throughout the South. During Congressional Reconstruction the southern states established public school systems with separate (segregated) schools for whites and blacks. In the years 1866–1870, the Freedmen's Bureau opened 4,239 schools, employed 9,307 teachers, and taught 247,333 pupils. During this same period the freedpeople contributed $785,700 to support their own schools. In 1870 roughly one fourth of black school-age children in the South attended public schools. This did much to combat illiteracy among the ex-slaves.

In August 1865, for example, Jourdon Anderson asked his ex-master whether schools had yet been opened for black children in Tennessee. Though he had many reservations about returning

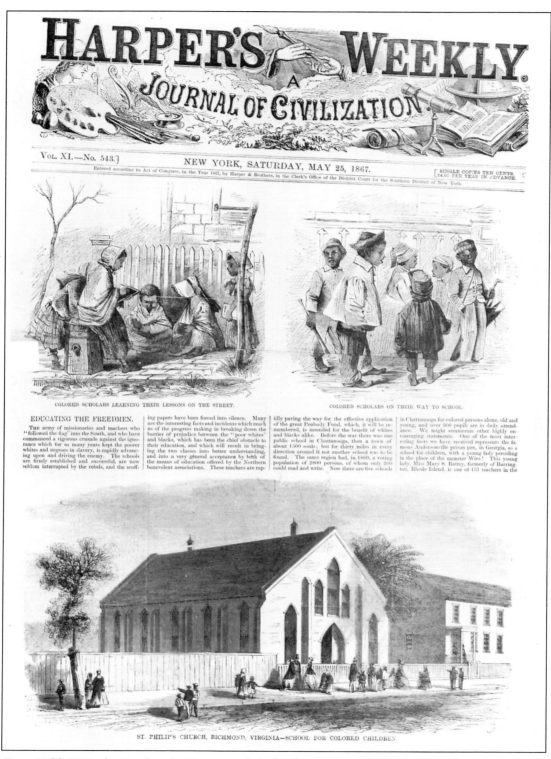

From 1866-1870, the Freedmen's Bureau and the freedpeople themselves—determined to exercise their right to an education—established thousands of schools throughout the South.

to the South and working for his former master, Anderson explained that "the great desire of my life now is to give my children an education, and have them form virtuous habits."[2] Schools for his children might have lured Anderson away from Ohio and back to his old plantation.

In 1866, Alexander Dunlop, a prominent black from Williamsburg, Virginia, informed a congressional committee that the freedpeople were determined to receive education. Though the black community was too poor to support schools, he assured the congressmen that they were firmly committed to providing their children with basic education. "They want it, and they have a desire to get it," Dunlop explained, "but the rebels use every exertion to keep teachers from them. We have got two white teachers in Williamsburg, and have got to put them in a room over a colored family." Black leaders feared that former Confederates would harm white educators who taught in freedmen's schools. Former slave Richard R. Hill agreed. He informed the committee that though tension existed between white teachers and ex-Confederates, the freedpeople in Hampton, Virginia, nonetheless were "anxious to go to school." Hill explained that "we have schools there every day that are very well filled; and we have night schools that are very well attended, both by children and aged people; they manifest a great desire for education."[3]

Many years after the Civil War, eighty-year-old Jasper Battle, an ex-slave from Georgia, recalled Reconstruction schools:

> School for colored chillun was held den in our church house. Our teacher was a white man, Mr. Tom Andrews, and he was a mighty good teacher, but Lordy, how strick he was! Dese here chillun don't know nothin' 'bout school. Us went early in de mornin', tuk our dinner in a bucket, and never left 'til four o'clock, and sometimes dat was 'most nigh sundown. All day us studied dat blue back

speller, and dat white teacher of ours sho' tuk de skin offen our backs if us didn't mind him. Dere warn't no fussin' and fightin' and foolin' 'round on de way home, 'cause dat white teacher 'lowed he had control of us 'til us got to our Mammies' doors and if us didn't git for home in a hurry, it was jus' too bad for us when he tuk it out on us next day wid dat long hick'ry switch.[4]

Though many of the teachers in the freedmen's schools were northern white ministers and missionaries, educated blacks also taught the former slave children. In New Orleans, for example, Dr. P. B. Randolph, a physician by training, served as principal of the Lloyd Garrison School. In October 1865, this school had seven teachers (five black, two white) and 373 pupils. Asking for help from William Lloyd Garrison, the North's most famous white abolitionist and the school's namesake, Dr. Randolph explained:

We are proud of our pupils, and feel that you will rejoice with us. We feel, also, that you will not take it amiss if we ask a little assistance from Boston in the shape of apparatus to illustrate astronomy ... a gyroscope and microscope, a numerical frame, conic sections, cube-root blocks, a magnet, and such other instruments as will enable us to fight this battle for our race against ignorance.[5]

Another black teacher, ex-slave Isabella Gibbons, began her school in Charlottesville, Virginia, in October 1866. At first she had forty-two students. But in less than two weeks she had enrolled sixty-three pupils. "The sphere into which I have been put into is so different from slavery," Gibbons marveled, "I hardly knew what steps to take; ... I read a chapter in the Bible ... I then told them I wanted [that they] should conduct themselves so as to reflect credit on the school and their race, in education, and by moral improvements." Gibbons was optimistic about the future work of the local Freedmen's Aid Society. Watching the freed-people learn to read and write, she believed that their "eyes had just been opened to see what education would do for them."[6]

Racial Segregation

Whereas blacks viewed education as a stepping-stone to real freedom, white southerners considered the idea of "educated" blacks a serious threat. Before the Civil War the South lagged behind the North in the development of common schools. Few whites—only the very rich—received formal education. As a result, during Reconstruction white southerners almost uniformly opposed providing state-sponsored schools for the freedpeople. They resented deeply the prospect of their former slaves becoming educated, possibly taking their jobs, and threatening their economic, social, and political status. After defeat in war and losing their slave property, whites were in no mood to educate the blacks. They also uniformly opposed integrated schools, where black and white children attended the same classes.

Not surprisingly, then, Douglass Wilson, a black Civil War veteran who lived in New Orleans, worried about how whites would treat his children when they went off to school after the city's race riot in 1866.

> We had no idea that we should see them return home alive in the evening. Big white boys and half-grown men used to pelt them with stones and run them down with open knives, both to and from school. Some times they came home bruised, stabbed, beaten half to death, and some times quite dead. My own son ... was often thus beaten. He has on his forehead to-day a scar over his right eye which sadly tells the story of his trying experience in those days in his efforts to get an education. I was

wounded in the war, trying to get my freedom, and he over the eye, trying to get an education.[7]

In 1867 the New Orleans *Tribune* observed that white Louisianans, even their Republican allies, opposed integrated schools. Just as whites had objected to the recruitment of black troops, emancipation, and black suffrage, they feared that integrated schools would break down the color line and weaken their power over the freedpeople. According to the editor of the black newspaper, those who sought to block integrated schools faced "the impossible task of conciliating a class of men who do not want to be conciliated." Blacks nonetheless were determined to send their children to schools with white children, he explained. Breaking up segregated schools would ensure that whites would "not be allowed to raise a class of rebel children."[8]

In 1872, Joseph H. Rainey of South Carolina, an ex-slave who served four terms in the U.S. House of Representatives, responded to a white colleague who feared that integrated schools might lead to full social equality between the races. What, Rainey asked, was so threatening about having a black child in the same classroom with a white child?

Now, since he is no longer a slave, one would suppose him a leper, to hear the objections expressed against his equality before the law. Sir, this is the remnant of the old pro-slavery spirit, which must eventually give place to more humane and elevating ideas. Schools have been mixed in Massachusetts, Rhode Island, and other States, and no detriment has occurred. Why this fear of competition with a negro? All they ask for is an equal chance in life, with equal advantages, and they will prove themselves to be worthy American citizens.[9]

Many years after Reconstruction, T. Thomas Fortune, a noted black journalist, recalled a racial incident that he observed during his boyhood in Marianna, Florida. In this town, as elsewhere throughout the South, the local black church housed the freedmen's school. As the black children walked to school each day, they passed an academy reserved for whites. The white children taunted them with jeers. At first the blacks ignored these insults. After several days, however, the whites began pelting the blacks with stones. According to Fortune, the blacks then prepared to do battle, arming themselves with stones and determined "to fight their way past the academy to their school." He explained:

> The colored children approached the academy in mass formation whereas in the past they had been going in pairs or small groups. [W]hen they reached hailing distance of the academy half dozen white boys rushed out and hurled their missles. Instead of scampering away, however, the colored children not only stood their ground and hurled their missles but maintained a solemn silence. The white children then seeing there was no backing down and scampering, as they expected, came rushing out of the four sides of the academy, and charged the colored children, who stood their ground stubbornly.
>
> During some fifteen minutes it was a real tug of war between them, with little ground given by either side. In the close fighting the colored children got the advantage, gradually, and began to shove the white children back, and . . . the white children broke away and ran for the academy. . . . There were many bruised on both sides, but none seriously, but it taught the white youngsters to leave the colored ones alone thereafter. They had enough fighting and never interfered again with the free going and coming of the colored school children.[10]

Though blacks during Reconstruction won individual battles and increased their literacy dramatically, whites kept them segregated in all areas of southern life. No longer excluded from schools, churches, hospitals, hotels, cemeteries, and public transportation, the freedpeople nevertheless were relegated to separate and unequal facilities. Racial segregation, first informal but later required by law, dominated race relations in the South for the next century. Unwilling to submit to such second-class citizenship, blacks complained loudly, bitterly, and forcefully.

Early in 1872, for example, a black Mississippian named "Civis" charged that whites were segregating railroads, schools, and riverboats in his state. "Civis" explained:

> It makes me blush when I see it, especially when the laws of the State confirm their right to travel in any car they please. Neither do the laws of the State prevent colored children from attending white schools,... but there are separate schools in almost every county in the State.... in this State, we are subject to most outrageous and inhuman treatment by the captains and agents of steamboats on the river; and it is on account of this, and similar treatment of our people in other States, that we wish to unite with thousands of our brothers in other parts of the country in petitioning Congress to give us relief.[11]

Based on such appeals, Washington's *New National Era* reminded its readers that the former slaves never would have full freedom until the U.S. government protected their political and civil rights. It must outlaw racial segregation. The editor explained:

> The blackman [*sic*] is not a free American citizen in the sense that a white man is a free American citizen; he cannot protect himself against encroachments upon the rights and privileges already allowed him in a court of justice without an impartial jury. If accused of crime, he is tried by men who have a bias against him by reason of his race,

color, or previous condition of servitude. If he attempts to send his children to the nearest public school where a free white American citizen, who pays no more taxes, can have the privilege without question, he is driven away and has no redress at law. If, after purchasing tickets for a ride in a first-class railway carriage, a colored person is hustled out into a smoking car, he or she has no redress at law because a custom prevails which allows injustice in this respect to colored persons.

In spite of emancipation, then, serious limitations on the freedom of blacks remained.

Also, in spite of the Reconstruction constitutional amendments, the newspaper editor complained,

We are not free. We cannot be free without the appropriate legislation provided for in the . . . amendments. We say to those who think we are demanding too much that it is idle to point us to the amendments and ask us to be satisfied with them and wait until the nation is educated up to giving us something more. The amendments are excellent but they need to be enforced. The result intended to be reached by the nation has not been reached. Congress has neglected to do its full duty.[12]

Convinced that only the federal government could stop the spread of segregation, blacks eagerly supported the Civil Rights Act introduced by Massachusetts Senator Charles Sumner in 1872. Bitterly opposed by Democrats, the U.S. Congress failed to adopt the legislation until after Sumner's death, in 1875. In its final form, the bill prohibited discrimination based on race in hotels, theaters, juries, and public transportation. Significantly, however, it fell short of outlawing segregation in schools and cemeteries.

James T. Rapier, a mulatto from Alabama who served in the

U.S. Congress 1873–1875, waited impatiently for Sumner's act to pass. In 1872, while traveling to Washington on a train, Rapier had been forced to ride in the smoking car and was refused food at train stations en route because of his color. He explained:

> I must confess it is somewhat embarrassing for a colored man to urge the passage of this bill, because if he exhibit an earnestness in the matter and express a desire for its immediate passage, straightaway he is charged with a desire for social equality, as explained by the demagogue and understood by the ignorant white man. But then it is just as embarrassing for him not to do so, for, if he remain silent while the struggle is being carried on around, and for him, he is liable to be charged with a want of interest in a matter that concerns him more than any one else, which is enough to make his friends desert his cause.

Rapier emphasized the public humiliation and constant embarrassments that blacks encountered while traveling in the South. He explained confidently, for example, that in Alabama

> any white ex-convict . . . may start with me to-day to Montgomery, that all the way down he will be treated as a gentleman, while I will be treated as the convict. He will be allowed a berth in a sleeping-car with all its comforts, while I will be forced into a dirty, rough box with the drunkards, apple-sellers, railroad hands, and next to any dead that may be in transit, regardless of how far decomposition may have progressed.

The situation was so bad, Rapier insisted, "that there is not an inn between Washington and Montgomery, a distance of more than a thousand miles, that will accommodate me to a bed or meal." He asked his fellow congressmen: "Is there a man upon this floor who is so heartless, whose breast is so void of the better feelings, as to say that this brutal custom needs no regulation? I hold that it does and that Congress is the body to regulate it." Rapier argued that "nothing short of a complete acknowledgment of my manhood will satisfy me. I have no compromises to make, and shall unwillingly accept any...."[13]

South Carolina's Richard H. Cain served in the House of Representatives during the debates over Sumner's Civil Rights Act. A shrewd theologian and politician, "Daddy" Cain urged Congress to pass Sumner's bill. "Spare us our liberties," he said, "give us peace; give us a chance to live; give us an honest chance in the race of life; place no obstruction in our way; oppress us not; give us an equal chance; and we ask no more of the American people."[14]

Responding to an anti-black speech by white Congressman William M. Robbins of North Carolina, Cain blamed whites for keeping the blacks suppressed.

> Yet these gentlemen come here and upbraid us with our ignorance and our stupidity. Yet you robbed us for two hundred years. During all that time we toiled for you. We have raised your cotton, your rice, your corn. We have attended your wives and your children. We have made wealth for your support and your education, while we were slaves, toiling without pay, without the means of education, and hardly of sustenance. And yet you upbraid us for being ignorant; call us a horde of barbarians!

Cain specifically questioned Robbins's assertion that under slavery, the blacks were not "ready" for education.

> How long would it have taken to get us ready under their kind of teaching? . . . How long would it have taken to educate us under the thumb-screw, to educate us with the whip, to educate us with the lash, with instruments of tor-

> ture, to educate us without a home? How long would it have taken to educate us under their system? We had no wives; we had no children; they belonged to the gentleman and his class. We were homeless, we were friendless.

Cain explained that the slaves, unlike the whites, lacked protection under the principles of the Declaration of Independence and the U.S. Constitution. Whereas the American flag symbolized freedom for whites, for blacks there were "no stars of hope . . . only stripes of our condemnation." Unfortunately, he added, long after the defeat of the Confederacy, blacks, especially women, remained vulnerable to white violence and abuse.

Finally, Cain objected to Robbins and other white racists who sought to rid the United States of the "Negro problem" by colonizing the blacks somewhere else. Cain declared that whites, not blacks, were responsible for slavery and ultimately must be held accountable for its consequences. He informed Robbins:

> You have brought us here, and here we are going to stay. We are not going one foot or one inch from this land. Our mothers and fathers and our grandfathers and great-grandfathers have died here. Here we have sweated. Here we have toiled. Here we have made this country great and rich by our labor and toil. It is mean in you now to want to drive us away, after having taken all our toil for two hundred years.

Cain, like most American blacks during Reconstruction, refused to leave the United States. This was their country, the land of their slave ancestors. The freedpeople were determined to carve out a place for their race here—as "part and parcel of this great nation." They were resolved neither to surrender to white racism nor to give up hope.[15]

Conclusion

RECONSTRUCTION AND ITS LEGACY

". . . the negro is still a slave."

Despite their determined attempts at political and economic advancement, black Americans struggled terribly during Reconstruction. They ultimately made limited gains and fell far short of true equality. In 1876 the ex-slave and black abolitionist Frederick Douglass addressed the Republican party's national convention. He thanked the whites for freeing his people but complained that because the freedpeople received no land, they suffered. "You turned us loose to the sky, to the storm, to the whirlwind, and, worst of all, you turned us loose to the wrath of our infuriated masters."[1]

Two years earlier, Lewis H. Douglass, son of the famous abolitionist and editor of the nation's leading black newspaper, regretted that "barbarism," the spirit of slavery, remained very much alive in the South. "There is," he said, "as strong a determination to keep alive a veneration for the institution of slavery, a feeling of hatred for the government for overthrowing the system, and of bitter prejudice towards the class of citizens from whom the manacles have been removed."[2]

Lacking education, money, and land, blacks confronted white racism at every turn. In addition to denying blacks the means to help themselves, whites used violent methods to maintain racial control. The Ku Klux Klan and other terrorist groups murdered, raped, and tortured the freedpeople and destroyed millions of dollars worth of their property. Whites intimidated the freedmen in order to keep them from the polls. When such tactics failed, whites resorted to election fraud to render black votes useless. During Reconstruction blacks thus were trapped into the conditions of neo-slavery by circumstance and by the determination of whites to dominate them.

Matters in fact got progressively worse for the freedpeople. During the 1870s northern Republican politicians in Congress gradually lost interest in their plight and virtually abandoned them. Soon the federal courts did too. Though the Civil Rights Act of 1875 outlawed discrimination by race in access to public accommodations such as theaters, trains, and inns, the Supreme Court in 1883 ruled in five cases that the 1875 statute was unconstitutional. The court argued that the Thirteenth Amendment outlawed slavery but was not intended to guarantee that former slaves be treated as equals to whites. It also declared that the Fourteenth Amendment was designed to protect persons against discrimination by the states only, not against private actions.

Justice Joseph P. Bradley, speaking for the majority, wrote: "When a man has emerged from slavery, . . . there must be some stage in the progress of his elevation when he takes the rank of a mere citizen, and ceases to be the special favorite of the laws." Bradley wrote that the 1875 Civil Rights Act gave blacks special

Reconstruction *by Thomas Nast.*

treatment, making them the "favorite of the laws." Justice John Marshall Harlan disagreed. He argued that unless the government secured their rights, blacks would remain defenseless against white attack. "The supreme law of the land," Harlan explained, "has decreed that no authority shall be exercised in this country upon the basis of discrimination, in respect of civil rights, against freemen and citizens because of their race, color, or previous condition of servitude."[3]

Lacking federal protection, from the 1880s onward blacks fell victim to white southerners who oppressed them at will. Whites found ways—some legal, others illegal—to deny the freedpeople schools, financial capital, and farms. Without these they could wield little political power. The freedmen, so hopeful in 1865, with dreams of "forty acres and a mule," found little to cheer about by 1880. Much of their enthusiasm was dashed because the government refused to compensate them for two centuries of un-requited toil. By the turn of the century, race relations in the South reached an all-time low. State after state segregated the races by law socially, economically, and politically. Between 1890 and 1920, whites lynched 2,523 blacks.

In 1903 the black scholar W. E. B. Du Bois described the condition of his people more than three decades after emancipation. Du Bois noted that

despite compromise, war, and struggle the Negro is not free. In the backwoods of the Gulf States, for miles and miles, he may not leave the plantation of his birth; in well-nigh the whole rural South the black farmers are peons, bound by law and custom to an economic slavery, from which the only escape is death or the penitentiary. In the most cultured sections and cities of the South the Negroes are a segregated servile caste, with restricted rights and privileges. Before the courts, both in law and custom, they stand on a different and peculiar basis. Taxation without representation is the rule of their political life. And the result of all of this is, and in nature must have been, lawlessness and crime.[4]

Seven years later Du Bois declared: "In many of the county districts of the South the negro is still a slave. The law protects him from being branded with the name of a slave. But the law allows him to be enslaved as a matter of grim fact and helps to forge the chains."[5]

Ironically, Reconstruction brought about little change in the day-to-day conditions of the South's poor blacks. To be sure, they were "free." But their "freedom" was far more limited than the slaves, and their northern white and black friends, had supposed it would become at the moment of emancipation. Tragically, the freedpeople's fertile hopes and dreams failed to take root. They were blocked again and again by whites who never could accept blacks as equals and resented their progress as a race. Despite their hard work and suffering during Reconstruction, blacks ultimately fell short in their attempts to be "free" in word as well as in deed. Though they attained limited success during Reconstruction, blacks nonetheless exhibited a sense of community, a group identification, during the emancipation experience. The black voices presented in this book attest to the strength, will, and resolve of a people who endured more than two hundred years of bondage.

These qualities eventually bore fruit. The blacks' quest for full citizenship, though delayed, finally arrived in the next century. True freedom for blacks came to pass during the Civil Rights era of the 1950s and 1960s. This time around, white northerners backed the black cause and the U.S. Supreme Court, drawing heavily upon the Thirteenth, Fourteenth, and Fifteenth Amendments for its decisions, championed racial justice. Significantly and quite properly, then, historians call this modern period the "second" Reconstruction. It was long overdue.

Despite this major triumph, in the 1990s racism continues to stain the fabric of American society, north and south. Subtle, and not so subtle, acts of segregation, racial injustice, and racial violence are common in education, housing, government, law, business, and the arts. Racism and intolerance lurk in the corners of American culture like an incurable social cancer.

Yet there are hopeful signs. Blacks occupy significant positions with distinction in every avenue of American life. They are leaders in politics, business, education, the military, sports, the trades, and the performing and visual arts. Recently, on March 16, 1995, Mississippi, a former Confederate state that declined to ratify the Thirteenth Amendment in 1865, finally joined the other states in officially banning slavery. Racial progress inches along slowly. But the black voices from Reconstruction nevertheless continue to resound.

Notes

INTRODUCTION

1. Dudley T. Cornish, *The Sable Arm* (1956; New York: W. W. Norton, 1966), 291.

CHAPTER ONE
THE PROMISE AND REALITY OF EMANCIPATION

1. Norman R. Yetman, ed., *Voices From Slavery* (New York: Holt, Rinehart and Winston, 1970), 99–100.
2. Ira Berlin, ed., *Free at Last: A Documentary History of Slavery, Freedom, and the Civil War* (New York: The New Press, 1992), 349.
3. Yetman, ed., *Voices From Slavery,* 320.
4. George P. Rawick, ed., *The American Slave: A Composite Autobiography, Volume 2: South Carolina Narratives, Parts 1 and 2* (Westport, CT: Greenwood Publishing Company, 1972), 5–6.
5. Berlin, ed., *Free at Last,* 310–314.
6. Ibid., 124–129.
7. Ibid., 265.
8. Ibid., 222–227.
9. Elsa B. Brown, "Negotiating and Transforming the Public Sphere: African American Political Life in the Transition from Slavery to Freedom," *Public Culture,* 7 (1994): 109, 113, 114.

CHAPTER TWO
CHANGING OLD WAYS

1. Norman R. Yetman, ed., *Voices From Slavery* (New York: Holt, Rinehart and Winston, 1970), 99–100.

2. "Review of the Work of the Freeemen's [*sic*] Bureau," January 20, 1870, 3:3–4.

3. Peter M. Bergman, *The Chronological History of the Negro in America* (New York: Harper & Row, 1969), 245.

4. Hans L. Trefousse, ed., *Background for Radical Reconstruction* (Boston: Little, Brown, 1970), 7, 8–9.

5. "Justice to the Negro," Washington *New National Era,* October 23, 1873, 2:3–4.

6. 46th Congress, 2nd Session, *Report and Testimony of the Select Committee of the United States Senate,* Part II (Washington: Government Printing Office, 1880), 192.

7. "Address from the Colored Citizens of Norfolk, Va., to the People of the United States," in C. Peter Ripley, ed., *The Black Abolitionist Papers,* 5 vols. (Chapel Hill: University of North Carolina Press, 1985–1992), 5:337.

8. Leon F. Litwack, *Been in the Storm So Long: The Aftermath of Slavery* (New York: Alfred A. Knopf, 1979), 334–335.

9. John David Smith, *An Old Creed for the New South: Proslavery Ideology and Historiography, 1865–1918* (Athens: University of Georgia Press, 1991), 31.

10. Ibid.

11. *Proceedings of the Colored People's Convention of the State of South Carolina* (Charleston: South Carolina Leader Office, 1865), 22, 23, 24, 25.

12. "Address from the Colored Citizens of Norfolk, Va., to the People of the United States," in Ripley, ed., *The Black Abolitionist Papers,* 5:337.

13. "The South as It Is, XIV," *Nation,* 1 (October 19, 1865): 493.

14. "Accepting the Past But Opposing the Future," New Orleans *Tribune,* December 21, 1867, 1:1.

CHAPTER THREE
REUNITING FAMILIES

1. Leon F. Litwack, *Been in the Storm So Long: The Aftermath of Slavery* (New York: Alfred A. Knopf, 1979), 232.

2. Ira Berlin, ed., *Freedom: A Documentary History of Emancipation, 1861–1867. Series II: The Black Military Experience* (Cambridge: Cambridge University Press, 1982), 665–666.

3. Ira Berlin, ed., *Free at Last: A Documentary History of Slavery, Freedom, and the Civil War* (New York: The New Press, 1992), 120.

4. Ibid., 103.

5. Ibid., 360.

6. Berlin, ed., *The Black Military Experience*, 779, 780, 781.

7. Berlin, ed., *Free at Last*, 228–229.

8. Berlin, ed., *The Black Military Experience*, 754–756.

9. Berlin, ed., *Free at Last*, 373.

10. Ibid., 375.

11. Norman R. Yetman, ed., *Voices From Slavery* (New York: Holt, Rinehart and Winston, 1970), 165.

CHAPTER FOUR

THE FIRST FRIEND: THE FREEDMEN'S BUREAU

1. Ira Berlin, ed., *Freedom: A Documentary History of Emancipation, 1861–1867. Series II: The Black Military Experience* (Cambridge: Cambridge University Press, 1982), 774.

2. "Review of the Work of the Freeemen's [*sic*] Bureau," Washington *New Era,* January 20, 1870, 3:3–4.

3. Ibid.

4. Hans L. Trefousse, ed., *Background for Radical Reconstruction* (Boston: Little, Brown, 1970), 4.

5. John David Smith, *An Old Creed for the New South: Proslavery Ideology and Historiography, 1865–1918* (Athens: University of Georgia Press, 1991), 221.

6. Ira Berlin, ed., *Free At Last: A Documentary History of Slavery, Freedom, and the Civil War* (New York: The New Press, 1992), 318–321.

7. Roger L. Ransom and Richard Sutch, *One Kind of Freedom: The Economic Consequences of Emancipation* (Cambridge: Cambridge University Press, 1977), 58–59.

8. John David Smith, "More Than Slaves, Less Than Freedmen: The 'Share Wages' Labor System During Reconstruction," *Civil War History,* 26 (September, 1980): 263–265.

9. "Review of the Work of the Freeemen's [*sic*] Bureau," January 20, 1870, 3:3–4.

10. "Justice for All," New Orleans *Tribune,* October 31, 1867, 1:1.

11. Trefousse, ed., *Background for Radical Reconstruction,* 12.

CHAPTER FIVE
A SECOND BONDAGE: THE PLANTATION SYSTEM

1. *Proceedings of the Constitutional Convention of South Carolina* (Charleston: Denny & Perry, 1868), 117, 354.
2. Ira Berlin, ed., *Free At Last: A Documentary History of Slavery, Freedom, and the Civil War* (New York: The New Press, 1992), 291–294.
3. Eric Foner, *Freedom's Lawmakers: A Directory of Black Officeholders During Reconstruction* (New York: Oxford University Press, 1993), 36.
4. *Proceedings of the Constitutional Convention,* 196–197, 379, 380.
5. "Kush," *The Political Axe for the Use of the Colored Men of the State of South Carolina in the Year 1872 with Constitution of the Progressive Association* (Charleston: n.p., 1872), 4, 5, 10.
6. Oubre, *Forty Acres and a Mule: The Freedmen's Bureau and Black Land Ownership* (Baton Rouge: Louisiana State University Press, 1978), 195.
7. "Emigration from Georgia," Washington *New National Era,* November 28, 1872, 2:6.
8. Painter, *The Exodusters: Black Migration to Kansas After Reconstruction* (1976; New York: W. W. Norton, 1979), 256, 257, 260.

CHAPTER SIX
ORGANIZING FOR EQUAL RIGHTS

1. *Proceedings of the Colored People's Convention of the State of South Carolina* (Charleston: South Carolina Leader Office, 1865), 25, 27.
2. Emma Lou Thornbrough, ed., *Black Reconstructionists* (Englewood Cliffs, NJ: Prentice-Hall, 1972), 25.
3. Ibid., 27–28.
4. "The Coming Convention," New Orleans *Tribune,* October 23, 1867, 1:1–2.
5. "Secure Your Rights," New Orleans *Tribune,* December 7, 1867, 1:1.
6. *Proceedings of the Constitutional Convention of South Carolina* (Charleston: Denny & Perry, 1868), 218, 724, 894.
7. Ibid., 830–831.
8. Ibid., 688–689.
9. Ibid., 726.

CHAPTER SEVEN
THE RIGHT TO VOTE

1. *Proceedings of the Constitutional Convention of South Carolina* (Charleston: Denny & Perry, 1868), 725.

2. "Important Petition to be Sent to the President," New York *Daily Tribune,* May 19, 1865, 6:3.

3. Augusta *Loyal Georgian,* April 10, 1867, 3:1.

4. "Acting Like Men and Being Treated Like Women," New Orleans *Tribune,* December 21, 1866, 1:1–2.

5. "The White Man Party and the Radical Party," New Orleans *Tribune,* October 30, 1867, 1:1.

6. "Is Disfranchisement Good Policy?" New Orleans *Tribune,* November 25, 1866, 1:1–3.

7. Ira Berlin, ed., *Freedom: A Documentary History of Emancipation, 1861–1867. Series II: The Black Military Experience* (Cambridge: Cambridge University Press, 1982), 822.

8. "Colored Voters of the South Take Heed," Washington *New National Era,* February 1, 1872, 3:7.

9. Mifflin Wistar Gibbs, *Shadow and Light: An Autobiography* (Washington: The Author, 1902), 141–142.

10. Emma Lou Thornbrough, ed., *Black Reconstructionists* (Englewood Cliffs, NJ: Prentice-Hall, 1972), 34–35.

11. "The Aim of Conservatism," New Orleans *Tribune,* December 14, 1867, 1:1.

12. Eric Foner, *Freedom's Lawmakers: A Directory of Black Officeholders During Reconstruction* (New York: Oxford University Press, 1993), xiv.

13. James S. Pike, *The Prostrate State: South Carolina Under Negro Government* (1874; New York: Harper & Row, 1968), 20–21.

CHAPTER EIGHT
THE FIRST LEADERS

1. "The Whipping Post," Washington *New National Era,* January 26, 1871, 1:5–7.

2. *Proceedings of the Constitutional Convention of South Carolina* (Charleston: Denny & Perry, 1868), 694–695.

3. "Negroes as Legislators," Washington *New National Era,* March 19, 1874, 1:4.

4. Emma Lou Thornbrough, ed., *Black Reconstructionists* (Englewood Cliffs, NJ: Prentice-Hall, 1972), 44.

5. Eric Foner, *Freedom's Lawmakers: A Directory of Black Officeholders During Reconstruction* (New York: Oxford University Press, 1993), 137.

6. W. H. Hardy, "Recollections of Reconstruction in East and Southeast Mississippi," *Publications of the Mississippi Historical Society,* 4 (1901), 126.

7. Foner, *Freedom's Lawmakers,* 215.

8. Edwin S. Redkey, ed., *Respect Black: The Writings and Speeches of Henry McNeal Turner* (New York: Arno Press, 1971), 31.

9. Thornbrough, ed., *Black Reconstructionists,* 52.

10. Foner, *Freedom's Lawmakers,* 61.

11. Ibid., 176.

12. *Proceedings of the Constitutional Convention of South Carolina,* 353–354.

CHAPTER NINE
RACIAL TERRORISM

1. Trelease, *White Terror: The Ku Klux Klan Conspiracy and Southern Reconstruction* (New York: Harper & Row, 1971), xi.

2. "Southern Brutality," Washington *New National Era,* July 30, 1874, 2:1–2.

3. "Report [of the] Select Committee on the Memphis Riot, July 25, 1866," *House Reports,* 39th Congress, 1st Session, vol. 3, no. 101 (Washington: Government Printing Office, 1866), 5.

4. Hans L. Trefousse, ed., *Background for Radical Reconstruction* (Boston: Little, Brown, 1970), 161.

5. "Report of the Select Committee on [the] New Orleans Riot, July and August, 1866," *House Reports,* 39th Congress, 2nd Session, vol. 2, no. 16 (Washington: Government Printing Office, 1867), 351.

6. Ira Berlin, ed., *A Documentary History of Emancipation, 1861– 1867. Series II: The Black Military Experience* (Cambridge: Cambridge University Press, 1982), 805.

7. Norman R. Yetman, ed., *Voices From Slavery* (New York: Holt, Rinehart and Winston, 1970), 114–115.

8. Emma Lou Thornbrough, ed., *Black Reconstructionists* (Englewood Cliffs, NJ: Prentice-Hall, 1972), 31–32.

9. "Affairs in Insurrectionary States: Report and Minority Views, Alabama, vol. 2," *Senate Reports,* 42nd Congress, 2nd Session, vol. 2, pt. 9, no. 41 (Washington: Government Printing Office, 1872), 1000, 1003–1004.

10. Hans L. Trefousse, ed., *Reconstruction: America's First Effort at Racial Democracy* (1955; Huntington, NY: Krieger Publishing Company, 1979), 138–146.

11. Thornbrough, ed., *Black Reconstructionists,* 46–47.

12. "From Georgia," Washington *New National Era,* September 10, 1874, 1:2–3.

13. Ibid., October 1, 1874, 1:6–7.

14. "From Tennessee," Washington *New National Era,* September 10, 1874, 2:4–5.

CHAPTER TEN
THE PROMISE OF EDUCATION AND A HOMELAND

1. James D. Anderson, *The Education of Blacks in the South, 1860–1935* (Chapel Hill: University of North Carolina Press, 1988), 18.

2. Leon F. Litwack, *Been in the Storm So Long: The Aftermath of Slavery* (New York: Alfred A. Knopf, 1979), 335.

3. Hans L. Trefousse, ed., *Background for Radical Reconstruction* (Boston: Little, Brown, 1970), 7, 8–9.

4. George P. Rawick, ed., *The American Slave: A Composite Autobiography, Georgia Narratives Parts 1 and 2* (Westport, CT: Greenwood Publishing Company, 1972), 68–69.

5. "Lloyd Garrison School—Colored," *Liberator,* 35 (November 10, 1865): 179.

6. "Extracts From Teachers' Letters," *Freedmen's Record,* 2 (November, 1866): 201–202.

7. Litwack, *Been in the Storm So Long: The Aftermath of Slavery,* 279.

8. "The Schools," New Orleans *Tribune,* October 24, 1867, 1:1–2.

9. "Education," Washington *New National Era,* February 15, 1872, 1:3–5.

10. T. Thomas Fortune, "After War Times: A Boy's Life in Reconstruction Days, Part 6," Norfolk (VA) *Journal and Guide,* August 20, 1927, 6:6–7.

11. "Civis," "Letter from Mississippi," Washington *New National Era,* January 18, 1872, 1:3–4.

12. "Give Us the Freedom Intended for Us," ibid., December 5, 1872, 2:2.

13. Emma Lou Thornbrough, ed., *Black Reconstructionists* (Englewood Cliffs, NJ: Prentice-Hall, 1972), 68–69.

14. Eric Foner, *Freedom's Lawmakers: A Directory of Black Officeholders During Reconstruction* (New York: Oxford University Press, 1993), 36.

15. Thornbrough, ed., *Black Reconstructionists,* 70–72.

CONCLUSION
RECONSTRUCTION AND ITS LEGACY

1. John W. Blassingame and John R. McKivigan, eds., *The Frederick Douglass Papers, Volume 4* (New Haven: Yale University Press, 1991), 442.

2. "The 'Barbarism of Slavery,' " Washington *New National Era,* April 2, 1874, 2:2–3.

3. Kermit L. Hall, William M. Wiecek, and Paul Finkelman, *American Legal History* (New York: Oxford University Press, 1991), 241, 242.

4. Du Bois, *The Souls of Black Folk* (1903; Greenwich, CT: Fawcett Publications, 1961), 41.

5. " 'Negro is Still Slave,' Declares Prof. Du Bois," Cincinnati *Times-Star,* December 5, 1910.

Sources

"Accepting the Past But Opposing the Future." New Orleans *Tribune,* December 21, 1867, 1:1.

"Acting Like Men and Being Treated Like Women." New Orleans *Tribune,* December 21, 1866, 1:1–2.

"Address from the Colored Citizens of Norfolk, Va., to the People of the United States." Ripley, C. Peter, ed. *The Black Abolitionist Papers, Volume 5.* Chapel Hill: University of North Carolina Press, 1992, pp. 334–343.

"The Aim of Conservatism." New Orleans *Tribune,* December 14, 1867, 1:1.

Anderson, James D. *The Education of Blacks in the South, 1860–1935.* Chapel Hill: University of North Carolina Press, 1988.

Augusta *Loyal Georgian,* April 10, 1867, 3:1.

"The 'Barbarism of Slavery.'" Washington *New National Era,* April 2, 1874, 2:2–3.

Bergman, Peter M. *The Chronological History of the Negro in America.* New York: Harper & Row, 1969.

Berlin, Ira, ed. *Freedom: A Documentary History of Emancipation, 1861–1867. Series II: The Black Military Experience.* Cambridge: Cambridge University Press, 1982.

Berlin, Ira, ed. *Free at Last: A Documentary History of Slavery, Freedom, and the Civil War.* New York: The New Press, 1992.

Brown, Elsa Barkley. "Negotiating and Transforming the Public Sphere:

African American Political Life in the Transition from Slavery to Freedom." *Public Culture,* 7 (1994): 107–146.

"Civis." "Letter from Mississippi." Washington *New National Era,* January 18, 1872, 1:3–4.

"Colored Voters of the South Take Heed." Washington *New National Era,* February 1, 1872, 3:7.

"The Coming Convention." New Orleans *Tribune,* October 23, 1867, 1:1–2.

Cornish, Dudley Taylor. *The Sable Arm: Negro Troops in the Union Army, 1861–1865.* New York: W. W. Norton, 1966 [orig. pub. 1956].

Douglass, Frederick. "Looking the Republican Party Squarely in the Face." Blassingame, John W., and McKivigan, John R., eds. *The Frederick Douglass Papers, Volume 4.* New Haven: Yale University Press, 1991, pp. 440–443.

Du Bois, W. E. B. *The Souls of Black Folk.* Greenwich, CT: Fawcett Publications, 1961 [orig. pub. 1903].

"Education." Washington *New National Era,* February 15, 1872, 1:3–5.

"Emigration from Georgia." Washington *New National Era,* November 28, 1872, 2:6.

"Extracts From Teachers' Letters." *Freedmen's Record,* 2 (November 1866): 201–202.

Foner, Eric. *Freedom's Lawmakers: A Directory of Black Officeholders During Reconstruction.* New York: Oxford University Press, 1993.

Fortune, T. Thomas. "After War Times: A Boy's Life in Reconstruction Days, Part 6." Norfolk *Journal and Guide,* August 20, 1927, 6:6–7.

"From Georgia." Washington *New National Era,* September 10, 1874, 1:2–3.

"From Georgia." Washington *New National Era,* October 1, 1874, 1:6–7.

"From Tennessee." Washington *New National Era,* September 10, 1874, 2:4–5.

Gibbs, Mifflin Wistar. *Shadow and Light: An Autobiography.* Washington: The Author, 1902.

"Give Us the Freedom Intended for Us." Washington *New National Era,* December 5, 1872, 2:2.

Hall, Kermit L.; Wiecek, William M.; and Finkelman, Paul. *American Legal History.* New York: Oxford University Press, 1991.

Hardy, W. H. "Recollections of Reconstruction in East and Southeast Mississippi." *Publications of the Mississippi Historical Society,* 4 (1901), 126.

"Important Petition to Be Sent to the President." New York *Daily Tribune,* May 19, 1865, 6:3.

"Is Disfranchisement Good Policy?" New Orleans *Tribune,* November 25, 1866, 1:1–3.

"Justice for All." New Orleans *Tribune,* October 31, 1867, 1:1.

"Justice to the Negro." Washington *New National Era,* October 23, 1873, 2:3–4.

"Kush." *The Political Axe for the Use of the Colored Men of the State of South Carolina in the Year 1872 with Constitution of the Progressive Association.* Charleston: n. p., 1872.

Litwack, Leon F. *Been in the Storm So Long: The Aftermath of Slavery.* New York: Alfred A. Knopf, 1979.

"Lloyd Garrison School—Colored." *Liberator,* 35 (November 10, 1865): 179.

" 'Negro Is Still Slave,' Declares Prof. Du Bois." Cincinnati *Times-Star,* December 5, 1910.

"Negroes as Legislators." Washington *New National Era,* March 19, 1874, 1:4.

Oubre, Claude F. *Forty Acres and a Mule: The Freedmen's Bureau and Black Land Ownership.* Baton Rouge: Louisiana State University Press, 1978.

Painter, Nell Irvin. *The Exodusters: Black Migration to Kansas After Reconstruction.* New York: W. W. Norton, 1979 [orig. pub. 1976].

Pike, James S. *The Prostrate State: South Carolina Under Negro Government.* New York: Harper & Row, 1968 [orig. pub. 1874].

Proceedings of the Colored People's Convention of the State of South Carolina. Charleston: South Carolina Leader Office, 1865.

Proceedings of the Constitutional Convention of South Carolina. Charleston: Denny & Perry, 1868.

Ransom, Roger L., and Sutch, Richard. *One Kind of Freedom: The Economic Consequences of Emancipation.* Cambridge: Cambridge University Press, 1977.

Rawick, George P., ed. *The American Slave: A Composite Autobiography, Volume 2.* Westport, CT: Greenwood Publishing Company, 1972.

Rawick, George P., ed. *The American Slave: A Composite Autobiography, Volume 12.* Westport, CT: Greenwood Publishing Company, 1972.

Redkey, Edwin S., ed. *Respect Black: The Writings and Speeches of Henry McNeal Turner.* New York: Arno Press, 1971.

"Review of the Work of the Freeemen's [*sic*] Bureau." Washington *New Era,* January 20, 1870, 3:3–4.

"The Schools." New Orleans *Tribune,* October 24, 1867, 1:1–2.

"Secure Your Rights." New Orleans *Tribune,* December 7, 1867, 1:1.

Smith, John David. "More Than Slaves, Less Than Freedmen: The 'Share Wages' Labor System During Reconstruction." *Civil War History,* 26 (September 1980): 263–265.

Smith, John David. *An Old Creed for the New South: Proslavery Ideology and Historiography, 1865–1918.* Athens: University of Georgia Press, 1991 [orig. pub. 1985].

"The South as It Is, XIV." *Nation,* 1 (October 19, 1865): 493.

"Southern Brutality." Washington *New National Era,* July 30, 1874, 2:1–2.

Thornbrough, Emma Lou, ed. *Black Reconstructionists.* Englewood Cliffs, NJ: Prentice-Hall, 1972.

Trefousse, Hans L., ed. *Background for Radical Reconstruction.* Boston: Little, Brown, 1970.

Trefousse, Hans L., ed. *Reconstruction: America's First Effort at Racial Democracy.* Huntington, NY: Krieger Publishing Company, 1979 [orig. pub. 1955].

Trelease, Allen W. *White Terror: The Ku Klux Klan Conspiracy and Southern Reconstruction.* New York: Harper & Row, 1971.

U.S. Congress. *Report and Testimony of the Select Committee of the United States Senate.* 46th Congress, 2nd Session, pt. II. Washington: Government Printing Office, 1880, p. 192.

U.S. Congress. "Report [of the] Select Committee on the Memphis Riot, July 25, 1866." *House Reports.* 39th Congress, 1st Session, vol. 3, no. 101. Washington: Government Printing Office, 1866, p. 5.

U.S. Congress. "Report of the Select Committee on [the] New Orleans Riot, July and August, 1866." *House Reports.* 39th Congress, 2nd Session, vol. 2, no. 16. Washington: Government Printing Office, 1867, p. 351.

U.S. Congress. "Affairs in Insurrectionary States: Report and Minority Views, Alabama, vol. 2." *Senate Reports.* 42nd Congress, 2nd Session, vol. 2, pt. 9, no. 41. Washington: Government Printing Office, 1872, pp. 1000, 1003–1004.

"The Whipping Post." Washington *New National Era,* January 26, 1871, 1:5–7.

"The White Man Party and the Radical Party." New Orleans *Tribune,* October 30, 1867, 1:1.

Yetman, Norman R., ed. *Voices From Slavery.* New York: Holt, Rinehart and Winston, 1970.

Further Reading

Abbott, Richard H. *The Republican Party and the South, 1855–1877*. Chapel Hill: University of North Carolina Press, 1986.

Berlin, Ira; Fields, Barbara J.; Miller, Steven F.; Reidy, Joseph P.; and Rowland, Leslie S. *Slaves No More: Three Essays on Emancipation and the Civil War*. Cambridge: Cambridge University Press, 1992.

Carter, Dan T. *When the War Was Over: The Failure of Self-Reconstruction in the South, 1865–1867*. Baton Rouge: Louisiana State University Press, 1985.

Cruden, Robert. *The Negro in Reconstruction*. Englewood Cliffs, NJ: Prentice-Hall, 1969.

Current, Richard N. *Those Terrible Carpetbaggers: A Reinterpretation*. New York: Oxford University Press, 1988.

——, ed. *Reconstruction in Retrospect: Views From the Turn of the Century*. Baton Rouge: Louisiana State University Press, 1969.

Finkelman, Paul, ed. *Race, Law, and American History 1700–1990: Volume 3: Emancipation and Reconstruction*. New York: Garland Publishing, Inc., 1992.

Foner, Eric. *Nothing But Freedom: Emancipation and Its Legacy*. Baton Rouge: Louisiana State University Press, 1983.

——. *Reconstruction: America's Unfinished Revolution, 1863–1877*. New York: Harper & Row, 1988.

——. *A Short History of Reconstruction*. New York: Harper & Row, 1990.

Foner, Eric, and Mahoney, Olivia. *America's Reconstruction: People and Politics After the Civil War*. New York: HarperCollins, 1995.

Gillette, William. *Retreat From Reconstruction, 1869–1879*. Baton Rouge: Louisiana State University Press, 1979, 1982.

———. *The Right to Vote: Politics and the Passage of the Fifteenth Amendment*. Baltimore: Johns Hopkins University Press, 1965, 1969.

Magdol, Edward. *A Right to the Land: Essays on the Freedmen's Community*. Westport, CT: Greenwood Press, 1977.

McFeely, William S. *Sapelo's People: A Long Walk into Freedom*. New York: W. W. Norton, 1994.

McPherson, James M. *Marching Toward Freedom: Blacks in the Civil War, 1861–1866*. New York: Alfred A. Knopf, 1967.

Miller, Randall M., and Smith, John David, eds. *Dictionary of Afro-American Slavery*. Westport, CT: Greenwood Press, 1988.

Perman, Michael. *Emancipation and Reconstruction, 1862–1879*. Arlington Heights, IL: Harlan Davidson, Inc., 1987.

Rabinowitz, Howard N., ed. *Southern Black Leaders of the Reconstruction Era*. Urbana: University of Illinois Press, 1982.

Smith, John David. "First steps to freedom: North Carolina's emancipation experience." *Tar Heel Junior Historian,* 35 (Fall 1995): 12–17.

———, ed. *Anti-Black Thought, 1863–1925*. 11 vols. New York: Garland Publishing, Inc., 1993.

Sterling, Dorothy, ed. *The Trouble They Seen: Black People Tell the Story of Reconstruction*. Garden City, NY: Doubleday & Company, 1976.

Trefousse, Hans L. *Historical Dictionary of Reconstruction*. Westport, CT: Greenwood Press, 1991.

———. *Lincoln's Decision for Emancipation*. Philadelphia: J. B. Lippincott, 1975.

Trelease, Allen W. *Reconstruction: The Great Experiment*. New York: Harper & Row, 1971, 1972.

Wesley, Charles H., and Romero, Patricia W. *Negro Americans in the Civil War: From Slavery to Citizenship*. New York: Publishers Company, 1967.

Index

About the Author

Dr. John David Smith is Graduate Alumni Distinguished Professor of History at North Carolina State University. He has written or edited six books and published more than fifty scholarly articles on slavery, the Civil War, and race relations in the United States.